THE NOVEL IN RUSSIA

THE NOVEL IN RUSSIA

From Pushkin to Pasternak

HENRY GIFFORD

*Professor of Modern English Literature in the
University of Bristol*

HARPER COLOPHON BOOKS
Harper & Row, Publishers
NEW YORK

To

Marc and Tania Wolff

This book was originally published by Hutchinson & Co. (Publishers), Ltd., in Great Britain and is here reprinted by arrangement.
First Harper Colophon edition published 1965 by Harper & Row, Publishers, Incorporated, New York.

LIBRARY OF CONGRESS CATALOG CARD NUMBER: 65–24655

Contents

CONTENTS

Introduction

'The crown of literature is poetry, and the Russians have not yet had a great poet. But in that form of imaginative literature which in our day is the most popular and the most possible, the Russians at the present moment seem to me to hold, as Mr Gladstone would say, the field. They have great novelists . . .'[1] Arnold in 1887, like most of his countrymen, knew nothing about Pushkin. Yet he is right in emphasizing the novel as the summit of Russian achievement (and Pushkin prepared for this). The great names in Russian literature which have become household words in the West are Tolstoy, Dostoevsky, Turgenev, Chekhov (for his plays more than his stories) and Pasternak (for his novel rather than his poetry). Pushkin, Lermontov, Tyutchev and Blok had no less distinction than the celebrated novelists; Pushkin indeed—and this is a paradox not many people outside Russia can accept—probably achieved more, as opener of the language and master of many forms, than Tolstoy or Dostoevsky. But Russian poetry from his day, though existing in its own right, has nourished the novel, so that the major line of exploration may be said to run through the novel in nineteenth-century Russia. It stems out of poetry, it meets poetry at various points, and in the twentieth century poetry for a while leads it forward. But this being a modern literature, inevitably in Russia, as in America, pride of place goes to the novel.

The comparison with America—Arnold initiates it, and Lawrence develops the idea[2]—is instructive in several ways.

[1] Superior figures in text refer to Notes and references (pp. 193-6

7

Russian literature has far more to show in the eighteenth century than American, and the protracted Russian middle ages are not by any means barren. Both, however, grew to manhood and independence at the same time (Pushkin knew and admired the work of his contemporary Fenimore Cooper); both stood in the same uneasy relation with Western Europe; both attained (in Lawrence's words) a 'pitch of extreme consciousness'. They are the two most modern literatures of our world, anticipating a hundred years ago the spiritual conditions in which we live. And both occupy themselves with defining the image and destiny of a people. They are directed towards the future, as though each nation foresaw in the nineteenth century that its days of plenitude and power still lay ahead. At the same time there are notable differences. The careers of Hawthorne and Gogol could hardly be more dissimilar, the one labouring for many years without recognition, the other instantly acclaimed. Melville in *Moby Dick* is the one novelist of the age to attempt the grand metaphysical scale of Dostoevsky; yet what corresponds in Melville's latter days to the extraordinary scenes when Dostoevsky spoke at the Pushkin celebrations in 1880? Emerson's funeral may have drawn out the New England farmers and their wives to bid farewell to an era, yet this kind of intimate bond existed in Russia not as a rarity but in the case of almost every considerable author. Russian literature, one has to conclude, counted for far more in the national life than did American.

The reason is largely political, since, as Chernyshevsky pointed out, literature took the place of free institutions.[3] The American novel was, in a sense, outside history: the Russian novel felt the bruise of history almost on every page. In nineteenth-century Russia the critics—men like Belinsky, Chernyshevsky, Dobrolyubov and Pisarev— wielded an extraordinary influence. Belinsky more or less decided for three generations the meaning of Gogol's work; Dobrolyubov made Goncharov's placid novel *Oblomov* and the discreet hints of Turgenev's *On the Eve* into live politics; Pisarev taught the young men of the 'sixties to imitate Bazarov in *Fathers and Children*. The Russian novel as Tolstoy or Dostoevsky wrote it fends off the political journalist with one hand and with the other reaches for religious truth. It belongs indisputably to its age; all the currents of thought and feeling at a particular moment press through it. And by the very passion of its commitment the Russian novel sees beyond the local and temporary into the nature of human life.

From *Eugene Onegin* (finished in 1831) to *Doctor Zhivago* (published in 1957) is a period of one century and a quarter —perhaps six generations. Already in 1877 Dostoevsky could claim for Russian literature a unique wealth of talent crowded into a small space of time.[4] The hundred years since *Onegin* are almost unrivalled in the whole history of literature for the energies then displayed by the writers of one nation. Seldom was a more vivid and copious record left to posterity. Now, while the echoes of that extraordinary time still vibrate, we can take its measure. The generations are linked by common anxieties and hopes; the same problems of national destiny, individual freedom, truth and justice 'stay on the agenda': for a hundred years Russian literature seems to be living through a single protracted crisis.

This had the effect of keeping past writers contemporary. A tradition is real when all its participants, the dead and the living, engage in a common pursuit. American literature of the nineteenth century has been defined as a continuous dialogue, and the same has been said of French literature.[5] But perhaps this comparison with a dialogue puts more stress on one kind of continuity—the logical unfolding of a theme by speakers separated in time—than on another kind even more significant—the continuity imposed by language. Any writer who uses a language has to define an attitude to his great precursors. It is more than a dialogue, then. Perhaps we should call a close-knit phase in literature, like that exemplified by the Russian novel, an emerging symphony, with contrasted movements and yet the closest dependence between every passage. The end does not lose sight of the beginning. In a dialogue parts of the argument may be demolished and drop out. But with living literature the past is carried into the present.

This book proposes to investigate the kinds of experience that the Russian novel was called upon to treat, and the qualities of imagination and language that it brought to bear on them. A view of the Russian novel, however arbitrary or incomplete, is also a view of Russian society as the individual found it. Literature mediates between the reality and the ideal, the imperfections of life and a 'possible other case'. Russia is to be judged not by her history but by her literature. It is here that we may read the commentary of a singularly candid people upon its own living.

PART ONE

THE TRANSITION FROM POETRY

I

Pushkin:
the novel in verse and prose

THE Russian novel begins in poetry, with Pushkin's *Eugene Onegin*. He worked on it from 1823 until 1831, during a decade when Russian verse still held the supremacy over prose. It could be argued that *Eugene Onegin* itself made good imaginative prose more possible by displaying the virtues of prose—'exactness and brevity', as Pushkin defined them in 1822. There are many aspects of *Eugene Onegin*, which was to initiate so much in Russian literature. The first and most important must be the quality of its language. The last two chapters show Pushkin's final ease and mastery; the Russian language comes fully into its own. It has been said by Pasternak that countless English idioms reveal the presence of Shakespeare, that the felicity of the language itself is Shakespearian. There can be no doubt that Pushkin blended his genius with that of the Russian language; he set upon it a character and a style which have lasted and are still to be sensed wherever good Russian is written. His candour, mobility, daring, restraint—these personal qualities provide the gold standard of Russian feeling. And it was he who, so far as any one man could do this, made Russian the vehicle for a great literature. Turgenev's tribute of 1880 is well known. He credited Pushkin with the accomplishment of two tasks 'in other countries separated by a century and more, namely to establish a language and to found a literature'. This was said at the unveiling of a monument to Pushkin in Moscow, when extravagant gestures might have been expected. But it only confirms what was said to Pushkin in a letter of 1825 by the poet Boratynsky:

> Our marvellous language is fit for everything; I feel this, though I cannot bring it to fulfilment. [The language] was created for Pushkin, and Pushkin for it . . . Lead Russian poetry to that degree among the poetry of all peoples, to which Peter the Great led Russia among the powers. Perform alone what he performed alone . . .

Two years later, when the third chapter had just been published, he wrote to another correspondent:

> About *Onegin* what is there to say! What brilliant diction, exact and free! This is the line of Raphael, the living and spontaneous brush of a painter of painters.

'Brilliant, exact and free': 'in him, as in a lexicon,' said Gogol, 'was contained all the wealth, force and pliancy of our tongue'.[1] There is no need to multiply tributes. Pushkin liberated the Russian language.

Onegin was planned as 'a novel in verse', between which and the prose novel there is, according to Pushkin, 'the devil of a difference'. The 'novel in verse' meant in those days Byron's *Don Juan*, boundless, endless and not often sublime. Pushkin's poem, although written by instalments, shows a formal perfection that the prose novel hardly attained before Flaubert. The manner may be casual and discursive, as in the first chapter which portrays Onegin the St Petersburg dandy and is itself dandified in tone. But the story will soon be found to have a careful design, originally in nine chapters grouped by threes, but later reduced to eight. The first three chapters present the three principal characters each in turn: I Onegin, II Lensky the poet, III Tatyana. These chapters form the exposition. The next three give the central action: IV Tatyana's declaration of love for Onegin; V the quarrel between Onegin and Lensky; VI their duel and Lensky's death. The last two chapters (between which would have been placed that on Onegin's wandering, now surviving only in fragments) provide the epilogue: VII Tatyana visits Onegin's deserted house and then is taken to Moscow; VIII Onegin's declaration of love for Tatyana in St Petersburg (the scene at the beginning) and his rejection.

This concern with form (not generally supposed to be characteristic of the Russian novel) is in no way arbitrary. It springs from the sensibility of Pushkin, disciplined by Voltaire's prose and delighting in apt contrast. And indeed the Russian mind, from the age of Peter the Great if not before, had been bred to antithesis: between Russia and Europe; Moscow and St Petersburg; the individual and the state. The modern novel depends on a contrast of manners. So when Onegin who has lived 'the fashionable life of a St Petersburg young man at the end of 1819'—note the precise dating—goes to take up his uncle's estate in the provinces, a drama of social and moral import presently begins. Sophisticated and impatient, he criticizes the dull inertia of *Rus'*, old rural Muscovy. But eventually it will be a woman loyal to its spirit, Tatyana, who is to criticize and dismiss him. When Onegin first succeeds his uncle he can piece together the old man's life—those forty years of squabbling with his housekeeper, staring out of the window and squashing flies—from the relics found in his room (II, iii). After Onegin's flight Tatyana visits the same room and there makes out from his furniture and books what kind of a man he is (VII, xvii–xxiv). This enlightenment prepares for the final scene in which Tatyana, once rejected by Onegin, now judges the man whose civilization is unequal to hers. She, a general's wife and made much of at Court, knows the emptiness of that society from which Onegin cannot break free. The books and wild garden of girlhood mean more to her than the 'fashionable house' (VIII, xlvi).

Pushkin's novel, like so many to follow it, is engaged with *mores*, as exemplified in the Larin family (they are well named after the Lares or household deities, and preserve 'the ways of our past', III, xiii); in village customs and superstitions (V, v–x); or in Tatyana's drawing-room (VIII, xxiii–xxvi). The national life—it comes almost to that—is viewed by an intelligence that combines irony with a power transcending it—the poet's spontaneous pleasure in human

variety, in the local and the characteristic. Pushkin's attitude to Russian society—even though Evgeny stands not
far from the Childe Harold of Byron, the Adolphe of
Benjamin Constant, and the Chatsky of Griboyedov in his
comedy *Woe from Wit* (1824)—improves on satire, because
the poet responds to a quality in Tatyana that eludes Onegin
—her imaginative sense of Russia. The Larins are protected
by her sympathy; so is Onegin. The appeal of Tatyana
validates her own world, both in the provinces and the
capital.

More than once in *Eugene Onegin* the poet hints at a
transition to prose; and what delighted Belinsky was the
frankness with which prosaic items—Onegin's fur collar
silvered by frost, the mud in Odessa streets—are presented
in the novel. This particularity had been gaining steadily
with Pushkin, and it is the mark of a novelist. The peasant
girls who are made to sing while they pick raspberries, or
the villager who gives his name when challenged in the
moonlight—'Agafon'—enter the story because with them
comes the breath of old Russia. So Evgeny's Breguet watch
or his straight and curved nail-scissors or the over-salted
pie at Tatyana's nameday party are there to touch in a way
of life. Pushkin enlarged poetry until nothing remained
foreign to it. One critic complained about 'the picture of
pots and saucepans etc.' at the time the Larins set out for
Moscow (VII, xxxi): 'We hardly supposed that these objects
could constitute the charm of poetry.' In fact the supreme
charm of Pushkin's poetry is its readiness to meet prose.
And prose had much to gain from the meeting.

Chapters VII and VIII of *Onegin* mark the final conquest
of style. They move with a precision and grace that even
Turgenev could not hope to emulate. In passages like the
following the Russian novelists went to school. Tatyana
and her mother have reached Moscow

> and now in St Kharitony's Lane the sledge halted at
> the gates before a house. They were at the old aunt's, ill
> in her fourth year of consumption. The door was flung

wide open to them by a spectacled grey Kalmuck, in tattered *caftan* with a stocking in his hand. They were met in the drawing-room by a shriek from the Princess stretched on her divan. Weeping the old women embraced, and exclamations flowed:

'Princess, *mon ange*!'

'Pachette!'

'Alina!'

'Who would have thought it? After such a time! Are you here for long? My dearest cousin! Sit down—how extraordinary it is! I declare, like a scene from a novel . . .'

(VII, xxxix–xli)

In a few minutes the old lady has to confess:

'Joy is bad for me now, not only grief . . . my darling, I'm no use at all . . . With old age coming life is just horrible . . .' And here, completely worn out, in tears she began a coughing fit.

(*Ib.*, xlii)

'Like a scene from a novel': she alludes to the sentimental romances of another day, but we can take the words differently. The Russian novel as we know it in the work of Turgenev, Goncharov and Tolstoy derives from moments like this.

The perfection of *Eugene Onegin* ruled out advance on the same lines. When Lermontov used its stanza for a brief tale, *The Tambov Treasurer's Wife* (1838), he imitated the very accents of Pushkin, as Turgenev did later in his verse tales. Both Lermontov and Turgenev found their own voices as novelists after they had turned to prose. The novel in verse could not be repeated even by Pushkin. Already in 1827 he was making a start on prose fiction (*Peter the Great's Negro*). 'The years incline me to severe prose', he confessed in the sixth chapter of *Onegin* (1826). This retreat of poetry from the narrative field was sudden and irreversible. When Walter Scott dropped his lays to write *Waverley* (1814) it meant more than the conversion of a mediocre poet into a considerable novelist. Within ten years Keats, Shelley and Byron had died: the next major poet would be Dickens. So in Russian literature: by 1840 prose fiction had a clear road, and a few years later Belinsky would proclaim that 'the novel and tale now stand at the head of all other kinds of poetry' (1848). Prose fiction is more accessible. As Pushkin himself reflected, 'has not poetry always been the enjoyment of a select few, while tales and novels are read everywhere and by all?' His own verse in the earlier 1820's drew as large an audience as any prose work (for instance, the very popular *History of the Russian State* by Karamzin). But when after 1825 its style altered, the common reader began to feel lost. Very soon the enlarged public of the 1830's (for which journalists like Polevoy were writing) made prose a necessity. It was only the prose novel that could muster a readership of all classes.

So Pushkin himself went over to the prose tale and short novel. In the beginning even such exquisite things as *The Queen of Spades* (1834) and *The Captain's Daughter* (1836) were judged (by Belinsky, for instance) a long way inferior to his poetry. When Pushkin published *The Tales of Belkin* in 1831 they fell virtually on deaf ears. It is true that Gogol profited from the *Tales*, and that long afterwards Tolstoy was to admire them; he called *The Queen of Spades* a masterpiece, as did Dostoevsky. Tolstoy even asserted that 'the best of Pushkin is his prose'. With that paradox few would agree. Even though subsequent writers had much to learn from Pushkin's prose, it must be reckoned a minor mode with him, and for at least twenty or thirty years his work in it was largely neglected; whereas *Eugene Onegin* laid firm hold on the imagination of later novelists. It was to provide, as one critic has said,[2] a formula: that of the fascinating stranger who gains the love of a naive and serious country girl, so that the confrontation is made between two sensibilities, two modes of living. The 'formula' is a situation which, once revealed, appears crucial; for three decades no other means so much, whatever the changes of detail, no other serves in the same way to energize the imagination. Pushkin had penetrated to the main issue, that of the 'superfluous man' set apart for good or ill from Russian society by his modern outlook. To state the case opened a whole range of possibilities, from Pechorin in *A Hero of Our Own Time* to Olenin in Tolstoy's story *The Cossacks*. But Pushkin also, by his management of its terms, by the adoption of a special tone, and the prompting of particular sympathies, set a tradition. His successors came to look at the situations, or others like them, with Pushkin's subtlety. Turgenev noted in him 'a peculiar blend of passion and calm', of intensity and detachment;[3] and this temper distinguishes all the writers who have learned most from Pushkin. The stanzas of *Eugene Onegin* have an unfailing tact: it is more than urbanity, one might call it purity of response. Pushkin harmonized not only the Russian language but also the Russian sensibility.

In prose he is naturally more circumscribed. Many readers have, like the young Tolstoy, found Pushkin's prose stories excessively bare and dry. It was his habit, in *Eugene Onegin* and elsewhere, to speak of a 'descent' to 'humble prose', even to 'despised prose'. You feel he is accepting a reduction, since the age demanded it. Pushkin's customary terseness which glides so buoyantly in *Eugene Onegin* seems almost a curt mannerism in his prose. The sentences are meted out in short independent clauses of six or seven words. They can have an austere beauty:

> The funeral was held on the third day. The poor old man's body lay on a table, shrouded and encircled with candles. The dining-room was full of domestics. They prepared to carry it out. Vladimir and three servants lifted the coffin. The priest walked ahead, the deacon accompanied him, chanting funeral prayers. The master of Kistenevka for the last time crossed the threshold of his house. They carried the coffin through the wood. The church lay beyond it. The day was bright and cold. Autumn leaves were falling from the trees.
>
> (*Dubrovsky*, 1832–3; I, v)

Here the brevity is in keeping; at other times the effect can be a little bald. Pushkin disliked the nervelessness of much contemporary prose:

> ... they never say *friendship* without adding: 'this sacred sentiment whose noble flame' etc. It should be: 'early in the morning'—and they write: 'Scarcely had the first rays of the rising sun illumined the eastern edges of the azure heaven . . .'
>
> (1822)

So he cut expression down to the bone. His own lyrical presence which had sustained *Eugene Onegin* is gone from the prose. Instead the style is neutral, or that of an assumed narrator.

The Tales of Belkin present five *anecdotes* each with its 'small straight *action*', a simple account of 'something that has oddly happened to someone'.[4] *The Shot* tells of a duel in two stages; *The Blizzard* of a miscarried wedding and the final recognition between the lost partners; *The Undertaker* of a nightmare in which the dead pay their respects to the man who has buried them; *The Station Master* of a seduced daughter and her father's decline through sorrow and drink; *The Young Lady Peasant* of a girl seeking her lover out in disguise. Similarly *The Queen of Spades*, which might have developed the subtlety of *The Aspern Papers*, also describing how an old woman is persecuted for her secret, remains a brilliantly told anecdote. (Belinsky is emphatic on this point.) Along with *The Tales* Pushkin wrote his four 'little tragedies'—in their way dramatic anecdotes, though more serious with the one exception of *The Station Master*. But whereas the dramatic pieces explore certain obsessions—avarice and jealousy, for example—only *The Queen of Spades* can be said to reveal much psychological finesse (in Hermann's hallucination). *The Tales of Belkin* make no enquiry; they state, and their undeniable beauty lies in the statement. Each story has its narrator, as the preface explains: a civil servant, colonel, shopman or young girl. None of the *Tales*, excepting again

The Station Master, is very significant in itself; they depend
on their presentation. And whereas the clarity and firmness
of outline are not lost in English, the ironies of inflection
are. Yet from the Editor's Preface onwards Pushkin is
engaged in parodying official styles and literary mannerisms,
and in critically defining the sensibility of each narrator
(as Emily Brontë does with Lockwood in *Wuthering
Heights*). *The Station Master* begins with a half-facetious,
half-pitying disquisition upon the lot of anyone who keeps
a posthouse: the narrator is clearly showing his quality.
But at the end every pretension falls silent:

> It happened in the autumn. Grey clouds covered the
> sky; a cold wind blew from the harvested fields, taking
> red and yellow leaves from trees on its path. I reached
> the village at sunset and stopped at the post house. Into
> the porch (where once I had been kissed by poor Dunya)
> a stout woman came and said in reply to my questions
> that the old stationmaster had been dead a year, that a
> brewer had moved into his house, and that she was the
> brewer's wife. I regretted my fruitless journey and the
> seven roubles spent for nothing. 'What did he die of?' I
> asked the brewer's wife. 'Drink, my dear,' she replied.
> 'And where is he buried?' 'Outside the village, next to
> his late wife.' 'Could I be taken there?' 'Of course you
> could. Hey, Vanka! Stop playing with the cat. Lead the
> gentleman to the cemetery and show him the station-
> master's grave . . .'
> . . . We came to the cemetery, a bare place without
> any enclosure, sown with wooden crosses unshaded by
> any tree. In all my life I had never seen such a forlorn
> cemetery.

So the visitor gives the little boy a coin

> and I regretted no more either my journey or the seven
> roubles laid out on it.

The whole episode might be called Chekhovian in its
poetry of the pathetic commonplace. This story had many

successors. It marks the beginning of a tradition in which 'the short and simple annals of the poor' would be recounted without glossing over the misery and the waste. Pushkin's humane feeling, too restrained to be sentimental, underlies this tradition.

He is the social commentator and historian of his own day in *Dubrovsky*, a study of rural despotism and a poor man's revenge, and in the many unfinished pieces left behind at his death. One of these beginning 'The guests had driven out to the summer villa' caught Tolstoy's eye in 1873 and immediately set him writing the first words of *Anna Karenina*. The beautiful young married woman in Pushkin's fragment occupies herself too much with an admirer:

> The stately Princess G. followed Volskaya with her eyes and murmured to her companion:
> 'This is extraordinary.'
> 'She's terribly flighty,' he answered.
> 'Flighty? That's nothing. Her behaviour is unpardonable. She is entitled to have as little respect for herself as she pleases, but society has not merited such disregard from her . . .'

Volskaya, like Anna, is not forgiven the breach of convention. The whole scene anticipates that which opens in the sixth chapter of Part 2 (Tolstoy's original starting-point), when Anna shocks Princess Betsy by her indiscreet behaviour with Vronsky. Another fragment ('At the corner of a little square . . .') sketches out the last phase in the relations between Vronsky and Anna:

> 'I'm not angry, Valerian: but it pains me to see how lately you have quite changed. You come to me as in duty, not at the bidding of your heart. You are bored with me. You are silent, you can't find occupation, you turn over books, you fasten on things so as to quarrel with me and go away . . . I don't reproach you: our heart isn't in our own power, but I . . .'

Valerian had ceased to listen. He was pulling at the

glove he had long since put on and impatiently glancing into the street. She fell silent with a look of restrained vexation. He pressed her hand, said a few meaningless words and ran out of the room, as a high-spirited school-boy runs out of class. Zinaida went to the window; she watched as his carriage was brought round, and he got in and drove away. For a long time she stood on the same spot, leaning her burning forehead against the frozen pane. At last she said aloud: 'No, he doesn't love me,' rang, ordered the lamp to be lit and sat down to her writing table.[5]

Pushkin's handling of aristocratic life, of scenes in drawing-rooms and in officers' billets, taught Lermontov, Turgenev and the young Tolstoy a notation which they used more fully but could scarcely improve. His interest in the world of station masters and undertakers directed Gogol to the same quarter. Lastly, his mock *History of the Village of Goryukhino* guided the satire of Saltykov-Shchedrin in his own *History of a Town* (1870).

Like other contemporaries of Scott, Pushkin had a very keen historical sense. Not only did he present his own time as current history (the St Petersburg young man *at the end of 1819*), but also he studied and wrote of the national past. His verse drama *Boris Godunov* (finished in 1825) dealt with the 'time of troubles' early in the seventeenth century. There were three crises in Russian history which occupied his thoughts: the upheaval caused by Peter the Great; the rebellion of Emelyan Pugachov (1773–5); and the invasion of 1812. The verse tale *Poltava* (1829) celebrates Peter the victorious commander in his public role; *Peter the Great's Negro*, a prose fragment of 1827, shows him in the work-shop and in the tavern. Ibrahim (Pushkin's own Abys-sinian ancestor thinly disguised) has returned from study abroad:

While they put to the horses, Ibrahim entered the post cottage. In the corner a man of tall stature, in a green *caftan* with a clay pipe in his mouth, was leaning on the

table and reading the Hamburg papers. Hearing that
someone had come in he raised his head. 'Ha! Ibrahim?'
he cried out, getting up from the bench. 'Welcome,
godson!'

(ch. ii)

Finally another verse tale, *The Bronze Horseman* (written in
1833), restores the legendary Peter, 'mighty master of fate',
who is first seen planning where his city will stand in the
Neva swamps, and then presiding over flooded St Petersburg, a bronze statue heedless of human suffering. Pushkin
considered the meaning of the year 1812 in a tenth chapter
for *Eugene Onegin* which proved too political to keep, and
only fragments of which survive. Twice he began a prose
story on this theme, and one of them, *Roslavlev* (written in
1831), foreshadows the supreme moment of *War and
Peace*: Napoleon's advance and the flight from Moscow.
The only work of historical fiction that he completed was *The
Captain's Daughter* (1836) on the rebellion of Pugachov.

Scott and his imitators in Russia and elsewhere saw
history as romance—'the poetry of the thing outlived and
lost and gone', to quote Henry James; though Scott also
had a concern with the sense of community and national
traditions.[6] Pushkin too liked to describe (in *Peter the
Great's Negro*) an old-world assembly and old-world
hospitality, just for their differences from his own day.
But there were intense preoccupations that brought him to
Peter and Pugachov and the year 1812. What had Peter the
Great signified for Russia?—a question that has never
dropped out of Russian literature, since October 1917
merely revised its terms. What caused the defeat of Napoleon? As he put it in *Eugene Onegin*:

The storm of the Year Twelve came—who helped us
here? The exasperation of the people, Barclay de Tolly,
winter or the Russian God?

(X, iii)

What lay behind the most terrible of peasant revolts in
Russia, when Pugachov, Cossack and sectarian, raised up

whole provinces against Catherine the Second? To answer
such questions Pushkin undertook massive research, preparing a *History of Peter* (unfinished), and in 1833 visiting
the scenes of the Pugachov rebellion to supplement the
knowledge he had already gained from the archives for his
History of Pugachov (published in 1834). Just as study of
Peter's reign issued in a poetic statement, *The Bronze
Horseman*, which converts the essence of history into
enduring myth, so *The History of Pugachov*, an exemplary
work of its kind, is subordinate to *The Captain's Daughter*.
The novel established the poetic truth about Pugachov.

It is *Waverley* in a Russian setting. The young officer
Grinyov once did Pugachov a kindness and so had his
protection when the reckoning came; to save Masha he
visits the pretender's camp and appears a traitor like
Shvabrin, his personal enemy who has gone over to Pugachov. But there are no agonies of divided allegiance for
Grinyov. As he says in Chapter 13, 'my conscience was
clear; I did not fear trial'. Pushkin had to spare him any real
involvement (although feeling strong human sympathy for
Pugachov) or the censor would have complained. So the story
of Grinyov remains a family anecdote: how he fell in love
with the captain's daughter, how they were separated after
the sacking of Belogorsk fortress, how he came back to
rescue her, and how she intervened to save him by pleading
with the Empress in his disgrace. Grinyov has blundered
into history, and escapes from it with relief. Thus far, the
pattern is purely Scott's. But for all that *The Captain's
Daughter* has much more impact than *Waverley*, and not
only because Pushkin never wastes a paragraph or a
sentence.

His attention to the rebel leader makes this a second and
deeper 'History of Pugachov'. From the moment that
Pugachov appears in a blizzard—Blok's symbol for revolution, here too it suggests elemental fury to come—the
focus of the book changes. Grinyov may be the nominal
hero but in fact he exists only for our better understanding
of Pugachov, who is to be, as the dream declares, his second

father and his protector. Pushkin has caught the Pugachov of popular imagination: a figure rather more sympathetic than the records warrant; and yet it may be nearer the truth. There is a blacksmith in *Dubrovsky* who can set fire to the house with his master's enemies inside, and yet go up on to the blazing roof for the sake of a kitten (I, vi). Pugachov too can be utterly brutal and yet to the boy who had once given him a warm coat he reveals his other self— the reckless Cossack who foresees the end, and lives spaciously. Grinyov's driver had not been able to tell whether the shape they saw in the blizzard was wolf or man. Pugachov may be both; yet to Grinyov he seems even pathetically human:

> I cannot account for what I felt on parting with this dreadful man, a monster and scoundrel for everyone but me alone. Why not admit the truth? At that moment a strong sympathy drew me towards him. I ardently wished to get him away from the scoundrels over whom he held command, and to save his head while there was still time.
>
> (XII)

In this image of Pugachov—violent, crafty, often exceedingly cruel, and then unexpectedly humane—Pushkin tries to make out the spirit behind those peasant risings that always threatened in a serf-owning country. Grinyov prays that he may never 'see a Russian rebellion, senseless and merciless' (XIII). And yet Pugachov, who must bear the main responsibility for so much horror, belongs to the people; he and his cut-throats are moved by the young Cossack's song about the gallows, 'a song of the common people'; he remains one of them, both in his wild excesses and in his stoical resignation at the end. Captain Mironov and his wife come closer to Pugachov, despite the difference in loyalties, than they do to their superior in Orenburg, General Rheindorp, who does not cease to tend his apples even when hearing Grinyov's terrible report. There is even a hint that Pugachov should be contrasted with the real empress, at least in their manners of granting a request. Pugachov acts freely on impulse; Catherine (as her responsibilities demand) must first look into the case before she can accede to Masha's petition. In spite of all, Pushkin betrays 'a strong sympathy' for the rebel leader. At the last moment Pugachov on the scaffold is said to have nodded in recognition to Grinyov. How much meaning are we to read into that nod? At least it re-establishes however faintly the bond between them, and Grinyov presently watches not a monster die but a human being. 'You see,' Pugachov had once told him, 'I am not so bloodthirsty as your sort say I am' (XI).

Belinsky called *The Captain's Daughter* a prose counterpart of *Eugene Onegin*. It has always taken second place to the novel in verse, and (in spite of Tolstoy) there is reason for this. *The Captain's Daughter* deserved far more notice than Belinsky gave it—one paragraph as compared with two entire chapters on *Eugene Onegin*. It is probably the finest historical novel in Russian except for *War and Peace*; and this exception shows that *The Captain's Daughter* is, after all, a minor thing. (Whereas *Anna Karenina* does not diminish *Onegin*.) Yet Pushkin brought to his prose novel a rare historical sense—one phrase will vivify an epoch and its manners; a grasp of the complexity in human affairs; and, as always, an almost miraculous sense of form and of the appropriate tone. Without Pushkin the nineteenth-century Russian novel would have wanted its guiding star.

2

Lermontov: *A Hero of Our Own Time*

LERMONTOV (1814–1841), the poet of a new generation, spoke to it with an authority allowed half grudgingly in Pushkin. The failure of the Decembrist conspiracy in 1825 bred a more explicit indignation, a heavier despair, than Pushkin had uttered; thinking men were more self-engrossed, at odds with society, bitter, impatient. Lermontov reflected this temper in his lyric poetry, which is often personal and accusing; but his work of profoundest effect was a prose novel, *A Hero of Our Own Time* (1840). In his Preface to the second edition (1841) he explained:

> A Hero of Our Own Time . . . is precisely a portrait, but not of one man; this is a portrait made up from the vices of our entire generation, in their full development.

And elsewhere in the same preface he said it had 'amused him to depict contemporary man'. Thus Lermontov's masterpiece explores for another *epoch* (such Belinsky insisted it was) the same questions that Tatyana had faced in Onegin's library. Its title proclaims the strength and limitation of Lermontov, as poet of his own time. Less versatile than Pushkin, he brought one side of Pushkin's achievement up to date: his novel is a variation on the last three chapters of *Onegin* (the duel; Onegin's wanderings; the final assessment). *Onegin* had a central place in Pushkin's mind throughout the 1820's; but *The Bronze Horseman* as a feat of genuine myth-making outsoars 'contemporary man': here notation yields to prophecy. Lermontov devoted a fine, concentrated gift to the problem that Pushkin had stated so luminously in *Onegin*. His imagination shows affinities with Pushkin's; to some extent the two poets inhabit the same territory.

The prose which, by way of earlier attempts like *Princess Ligovskoy* (begun 1836), Lermontov had perfected for this summary work of his career grew inevitably out of Pushkin's. Most important for Lermontov was the example of such commentaries on fashionable life as *The Queen of Spades* and some of the fragments admired by Tolstoy. Lermontov followed Pushkin in seeking simplicity. There is a passage in *Princess Ligovskoy* where he defines the 'good tone' of a select circle much as Pushkin had done when he described Tatyana's salon. Lermontov would like a drawing-room

> where clever and varied conversation replaces dancing
> (let alone routs), where one may speak of everything . . .
>   (II)

and free play is allowed to thought and feeling. The ideal of such conversation governs his prose, as it had Pushkin's; the characteristic tone (found in Pechorin's journal, when the 'hero of his time' speaks to us directly) is moderated by irony: it never becomes loud or sensational, making an assault on the reader. Lermontov's narrative voice is at once candid and impersonal. It has the distinction of good breeding, as he and Pushkin conceived this: a deliberate negligence, at times an assumed remoteness. The ideal of manners that both held (and it should not be overlooked in the case of Tolstoy) required that speech should be lively and unrestrained. It must have the freedom of an intimate circle, where affectation will be derided (as Pechorin derides it in Grushnitsky) and emphasis depends upon tact. The result is a natural prose with the grace of perfect control.

Lermontov achieved this control simultaneously in verse and prose. As Belinsky observes, he was equal to himself in both. The brief verse epistle (*Valerik*), on a skirmish with Caucasian hillmen at which he had been present (dated 1840), probably did as much for Tolstoy, in showing him how to write the objective story of war, as Lermontov's prose in exemplifying the way of psychological truth. The same year, 1840, saw the publication of his prose novel, *A Hero of Our Own Time*. Whereas the profoundest things were said by Pushkin in verse, a moment of equilibrium had now arrived, and Lermontov could choose either mode. That he made his most rounded statement in prose at least proves that the medium was now ready. For some fifteen years the novel had been searching for an adequate prose. This Pushkin had gone a long way towards providing; and the first major talent committed to prose, that of Gogol, was already at work. Belinsky regarded the shift as rational. It meant for him an extension of poetry from the lyrical and subjective to a new range of possibilities, or, as he put it differently, a bringing together of poetry and life. Nothing had been clearer in Pushkin's poetic career than his gradual emancipation from strict forms (achieved in the main through *Eugene Onegin*) and his mingling of styles. In the prose novel it might be said that the principal kinds (lyric, epic and drama) met together: the frontiers were down. Belinsky counted this a sign of progress in literature, because 'actuality' could be made present in greater force. The tendency of Lermontov's day was to transfer more and more values into the keeping of prose. *A Hero of Our Own Time* made the necessary link between *Onegin* and the Russian prose novel in its maturity.

Yet the range has become, at this point, narrower. *Onegin* had two principals, the hero himself and Tatyana, each representing a metaphysic. There is attraction and conflict between them; and the metaphysic of Tatyana, the values that she denotes, finally triumph. On the way to this conclusion, Pushkin takes licence for much incidental satire upon mediocrity wherever placed. In Lermontov's scheme one of the protagonists and hence the alternative metaphysic are virtually missing. Interest gathers upon Pechorin himself, the dark flower of a generation. The whole book is a study of Pechorin, or rather a group of studies variously effected and complementary. First, the old staff-captain Maxim Maximych recounts an episode in Pechorin's life, the abduction of Bela, a local chief's daughter, in the Caucasus. Next, the author, who has become curious about Pechorin from the faithful but also limited reflection of him in this narrative, meets the man himself, and witnesses his detached way with Maxim Maximych. Finally, from Pechorin's journal, he copies down three further episodes. The first, amounting to little in itself, but beautifully evocative, tells how Pechorin was once robbed by a blind boy and nearly drowned by a girl smuggler. The second is Pechorin's most complete revelation, and follows day by day the vicissitudes of a double love story. The third, a mere appendage and yet, as Belinsky said, necessary for a full understanding of Pechorin, is an anecdote on the theme of fatality. Thus all five parts, but the central one, 'Taman', to a lesser degree, disclose the mind and heart of Pechorin; and even 'Taman' shows his sensibility to sea and moonlight and to the elusive girl.

Our business is with Pechorin, and others figure in the story for the main purpose of drawing him out. If Pechorin were simply, like Byron's Corsair or his Lara, an energy, a rampant will and no more, the effect would be monotonous. At times he does represent himself as sheer will:

> I look on the sufferings and joys of others merely in relation to myself, as a food that sustains my spiritual forces . . . My first satisfaction is to subject to my will everything that surrounds me: to arouse towards oneself a feeling of love, devotion and awe—is that not the first sign and the greatest triumph of dominion?
>
> ('Princess Mary', 11 June)

Happiness is for him 'sated pride'; which can be a very tedious state of mind. However, Pechorin's pride is sometimes in jeopardy: the will struggles with conscience, and the value of knowing Pechorin, other than as an example in a historical casebook, derives from the sensibility that he displays. He is put before us as an intelligence, strong but occasionally in the dark; seeking to realize itself in adverse conditions; following and not guiding the will.

'In me there are two men: one lives in the full meaning of the word, the other thinks and judges him' (*Ib.*, 27 June). So Pechorin confesses to Werner on their way to the duel. The man who acts, when he is confronted by the insolent treachery of Grushnitsky, feels 'the vexation of affronted self-love, and contempt, and hatred'; he enjoys bringing down the whole structure of his enemies' falsehood and intrigue; in the pursuit of revenge, he smothers his conscience. But after Grushnitsky is dead, the reflective man has to acknowledge:

> A stone weighed on my heart. The sun seemed to me dim, its rays did not warm me.
>
> (*Ib.*, 27 June)

The man who lives fully delights in a challenge to his will— is it to possess Bela? to find out the smugglers' secret? to infatuate a young girl, and to confound his enemies? to overpower a drunkard gone berserk? He likes trying his fate. By throwing all his energies into some kind of gamble he can prove to himself that he is fully alive. Pechorin seems always in quest of validation.

> Yesterday I arrived in Pyatigorsk, and took quarters on the edge of the town, at the highest point by the foot of Mashuk: in time of storm the clouds will descend to my roof. Today at five in the morning, when I opened the window, my room was filled with the scent of flowers growing in a little plot behind rails. Branches of flowering cherry look in at me through the windows, and the breeze now and again sprinkles my writing table with their white petals. I have on three sides a superb view . . . What happiness to live in a land like this! A pleasurable feeling courses through all my veins. The air is pure and fresh, like a child's kiss; the sun brilliant, the sky dark blue—what more could one need? what have passions, desires, regrets to do here? . . . However it is time. I shall go to the Elizabeth Spring: there, they tell me, is

gathered each morning all the society of the watering place.

(Ib., 11 May).

For one moment he seems to have found what Lawrence calls a 'trembling *balance*' between himself and the universe. The balance, of course, is deceptive, if only because he must go off in pursuit of passions, desires, regrets, to where society meets. But it is otherwise untrue. Pechorin welcomes the scene as ministering to his senses (a thrill in the blood) and to love of dominion ('at the highest point . . . I have on three sides a superb view'). The flowers and the air's innocence cannot be let alone. He will own subsequently to

> an immeasurable satisfaction in possessing a young spirit that has scarcely unfolded itself. It is like a flower, the finest scent of which is exhaled on meeting the first ray of the sun; you must pluck it this very moment and, when you have smelt your fill, toss it on to the road: perhaps someone will pick it up.

(Ib., 11 June)

Later, when all has ended in bloodshed and disillusion Pechorin slowly recognizes that nature is not simply for him: he comes to his senses in the bare steppe. And finally, with the last of his recorded experiences, walking home after Vulich has made a trial of destiny, he is brought to a metaphysical insight. The stars shine on, indifferent to man: Pechorin has at last taken measure of a universe that he cannot dominate.

Towards the definition of this character Lermontov had been working more or less single-mindedly throughout his career. Pechorin matters to Lermontov because their experiences are very close; but the task of rendering and explaining him had a broad object in view, to enlighten a generation.

> Reading over these notes, I was convinced about the sincerity of one who has so mercilessly exposed his own weaknesses and vices. The history of a human spirit,

even the meanest spirit, is probably more curious and profitable than the history of an entire people, particularly when it is the result of observation by a mature mind of itself and when it is written without the vainglorious wish to awaken sympathy or admiration. Rousseau's confession has the defect that he read it to his friends.

(Preface to 'Pechorin's Journal')

Pechorin is remarkably truthful. He accuses himself of being 'morally a cripple'; the 'inevitable character of Act Five', always 'an executioner or a traitor'; he has 'played het role of a hatchet in the hands of fate'. One thing he can never give up, his independence; he is afraid of being laughed at; the feelings have gone dead in him. The 'man who thinks and judges' is not deceived. Pechorin may offer excuses, telling Mary

I was prepared to love the whole world—nobody understood me; and I studied to hate.

('Princess Mary', 11 June)

Or he explains himself as the roving pirate who feels aimless on shore, away from the congenial tempest. But the last word is not left with Pechorin. Morality is tested by actions: the interest of the book naturally lies in Pechorin's behaviour, of which his explanations are tentative. Lermontov may have summoned the other characters either as subjects for Pechorin's ambition, or as witnesses to his conduct; but they live their proper lives: Maxim Maximych cannot suppress his tears when rebuffed by Pechorin at their meeting which the author observes; Mary when rejected by him goes through an agony of shame and eventual hatred that gives her (in George Eliot's term) 'an equivalent centre of self'. There is then, for all the concentration upon Pechorin, a spirit of justice—a genuine breadth of sympathy —in the book. Pechorin's case stands not on its own but is shaped and modified by other lives that impinge. Lermontov sees it with a novelist's eye in relation.

His disclosure of the complete man proceeds by stages.
Truth accumulates: it is a progressive portrait. And thus
no one account can be taken as absolute. Pechorin's self-
scrutiny in the journal puts him under the bleakest and
clearest light, but his own report on this episode with an
old flame and a new victim, however sincere, needs to be
set against evidence from outside. Before this, accordingly,
he is reflected for the reader in the troubled mind of Maxim
Maximych, whose simple beliefs and attitudes at once
provide the norm and are ironically questioned; he submits
for a few minutes to inspection from the author himself,
who notes the controlled hands, the unsmiling eyes; and
finally those three 'honest freebooters' of Taman, when he
breaks into their business, see him for what he is, a menace
to quiet lives. These various views of Pechorin, soon to be
amplified by his own revelations, do more than excite
curiosity. They show the 'hero of his own time' in the
relations that the time contributes. Even if Pechorin's past
is unsounded, and his death elsewhere dryly affirmed, those
tracts of his experience that bear the light are dense in
relations. With Maxim Maximych, with the boy Azamat
and the hillman Kazbich, as with Bela, Vera and Princess
Mary, with Werner and Grushnitsky and the fire-eating
dragoon, with Vulich and the officers of his regiment,
Pechorin is more or less passionately involved. He lives
under the conditions that a novel is best equipped to
investigate. And the time no less than its hero must be
studied, they are in such close and uneasy union.

Lermontov's sympathy for Maxim Maximych brings
about a complication of values. The author, not yet at
home in the Caucasus, has to respect this veteran for his
shrewdness about ox-drivers and weather portents. Meeting
him thus at the start, and hearing the story from his lips,
inevitably he concedes to Maxim Maximych a place in the
foreground. Through the staff-captain's talk a whole way
of life (already familiar in part from the garrison of Belogorsk in *The Captain's Daughter*) stands forward unself-
consciously to be judged. He is in possession not only of a

story which the author has to cajole from him, but also of the complete Caucasian experience. In telling his reminiscences he makes over, by instalments, the full truth of his being—the civilization in which he lives. Much as Ellen Dean in *Wuthering Heights* communicates what she knows of Heathcliff, and seeks to counter his strangeness with her traditional lore, Maxim Maximych faces Pechorin in the strength of a lifetime's convictions—and, like Ellen Dean, has to admit defeat:

He lay in the first room on the bed, one arm propping his neck, the other holding a pipe that had gone out. The door to the second room was locked, and no key was visible . . . I began to cough and strike my heels on the threshold, but he pretended not to hear.

'Ensign,' I said as severely as possible. 'Do you not see that I have come to you?'

'Ah, hallo, Maxim Maximych! Would you care for a pipe?' he answered without getting up.

'Excuse me. I am not Maxim Maximych: I am the staff-captain.'

'It's all the same. Would you like tea? If only you knew how tormented I am by worry!'

'I know everything,' I replied, going up to the bed.

'So much the better: I'm not in the mood to tell the whole story.'

'Ensign, your conduct is such that I may be called on to answer for it . . .'

'Enough. What harm in that? We've long since gone shares in everything.'

'Are you joking? Kindly give me your sword.'

'Mitka, my sword.'

Mitka brought the sword. Having performed my duty, I sat on his bed, and spoke to him:

'Listen, Grigory Alexandrovich, confess that it's wrong.'

'What's wrong?'

'Why, your taking Bela . . . What shall I do with that brute Azamat? . . . Now, confess,' I said to him.

'But if I like her?'

Well, what would you have me answer to that? I was
properly caught . . .

('Bela')

And in the discussion that follows he is again caught, until
finally he protests that 'there are people with whom you are
absolutely compelled to agree'. The official visit, with sword
and epaulettes, has meant nothing. Maxim Maximych, like
Ellen Dean, learns to capitulate. There are situations in
which common sense is disarmed.

It would be wrong to suppose that Lermontov asserts
the moral superiority of Maxim Maximych over Pechorin,
or that when Pechorin cuts short the old man's effusive
welcome on their meeting again he is necessarily at fault.
His manner may be heartless, but honesty forbids him to
revive what now lies dead and beyond recall. Lermontov
has shown Maxim Maximych in his quality—simple,
generous, loyal, sympathetic—but there is a tragic impossi-
bility of friendship between him and Pechorin. The aim of
this novel was not, as Lermontov said in his Preface, to
correct vices but to tell bitter truths. The balance of approval
does not come down on Maxim Maximych's side, as in
Onegin it did on Tatyana's. Pechorin is an uncommon
man; Maxim Maximych has the common virtues: but these,
unfortunately, turn to insipidity and worse when they are
transplanted. The hectoring dragoon captain also lives by
the soldier's code; so does Grushnitsky.

Pechorin gains salience from each one of his encounters.
Werner, for example, might seem to be almost a second
self; but this caustic, aloof doctor is shaken by Pechorin's
inhuman calm and ruthlessness in the duel: he cannot, like
Pechorin, 'take on himself the full burden of responsibility'.
No ordinary man is equal to Pechorin, as Vera testifies in
her last letter:

She who has once loved you cannot look without a
certain contempt upon other men, not because you are
better than they, far from it; but in your nature there is

something special, belonging to you alone, something
proud and mysterious . . .

('Princess Mary', 27 June)

It should be noted that Lermontov does not himself 'look
with contempt upon other men'. When they are false and
shallow, like Grushnitsky and the dragoon captain, they
deserve the scorn of Pechorin and by implication of Lermontov. Against Grushnitsky's posture of mysterious suffering
and banal heroism the genuine humanity in Pechorin and
his awareness of others are made visible. Nobody in this
book passes unnoticed: they all get their due, even Grushnitsky who shows the courage of consistency in his last
moments.

It is, of course, by the author's own general awareness,
and not simply by his apprehension of a particular type at
a particular moment, that the work survives. Pechorin's
candour has exemplary value: the comments that drop
from him sometimes attain a Stendhalian clarity; and of all
the 'superfluous men' in which Russian literature abounds,
he shares with Griboedov's Chatsky the distinction of
possessing a real mind. As Belinsky saw, he comes very
close to Lermontov himself, almost to the degree that
Levin represents Tolstoy; and Lermontov's feat was to
separate Pechorin from his own interests, to judge and
transcend him. For the intelligence that pervades the whole
book is Lermontov's, not Pechorin's: wider in sympathy,
more attentive to those who, like Maxim Maximych, are
nonentities in Pechorin's view; an intelligence that can
grasp the whole of relations, understanding the time that
has shaped its hero.

One rests on the perfection of Lermontov's prose. Whether
he is describing the solemnity of a mountain journey—

There was an utter stillness in the sky and on earth, as
in a human heart at the instant of morning prayer; only
at rare intervals a cool wind came in from the east,
lifting the horses' manes which were covered in hoar-frost

('Bela')

—or the girl at Taman who resembles Goethe's Mignon, or that last scene with Mary, the expression never fails in its cool elegance:

> I stood facing her. We were long silent; her large eyes, filled with an inexpressible grief, so it seemed, searched in mine for something like hope; her pale lips tried vainly to smile; her soft hands, folded upon her knees, were so thin and transparent that I pitied her.
>
> ('Princess Mary', 27 June)

Lermontov writes like Pushkin, with the same control over his feelings, the same ease of definition; only his sentences are more subtly harmonized; he is genuinely ambidextrous. Like Pushkin, he fashions a prose responsive to many voices (the strongly grained soldier's talk of Maxim Maximych, the blind boy's slippery Ukrainian, Grushnitsky's declamatory vein); and he achieves the same positive but impersonal style in his narrative. Tolstoy's *Cossacks* and such impressions of military life as *The Wood Cutters* deepen and refine the renderings of it that Lermontov had already made. For the foreign reader at large he signifies less in his own right than as the precursor of Tolstoy— sensuous, keen-eyed and sympathetic towards the plain soldier. He was also an original force in Russian literature, with a distinct impress of his own, moulding his thought classically and gauging the proportions of truth.

3

Gogol's *Dead Souls*

ON GOGOL's death Turgenev wrote: 'You have to be a Russian to understand whom we have lost. . . .' 'The most penetrating minds among foreigners,' he asserted in the same letter, 'for example Mérimée, have seen in Gogol merely a humorist in the English manner. His historical significance altogether eludes them.'[1] It was this 'historical significance' that caused Gogol (1809–1852) so much grief and perplexity. One cannot discuss Gogol's work without reference to Belinsky, who fostered for him a reputation he could not live up to. Following Belinsky, another critic of wide influence, Chernyshevsky, referred to the 1840's as 'the Gogol period in Russian literature'. It would seem that Gogol was allotted a role somewhat beyond his means. At that time he was a necessary writer, the conscripted spokesman of a tendency that he never came fully to understand. With him began the long reign of 'critical realism', of the 'natural school', as Belinsky named it, and for many readers Gogol was more important than Pushkin.

To recapture the first enthusiasm we may turn to the recollections of the music and art critic Stasov. In the summer of 1842 when *Dead Souls* appeared he and his school friends read it aloud by turns. They had known for some years Gogol's St Petersburg tales, rich in fantasy and pathos, his absurd sketches of country gentlemen, and his comedy *The Inspector General* which, like the cartoons of Daumier, made the official world suddenly and for ever grotesque. In *Dead Souls* they recognized something of the highest originality, a work 'incomparably national'. Gogol had already delighted them with his language, so fresh and

40

sly and various; 'all the young people began to speak
Gogol's idiom'; and now from *Dead Souls* they received a
whole lexicon of winged words, apt and mocking.[2] The early
Dickens gave his countrymen similar household phrases,
but Gogol's effect lies more inextricably in his own language.
Dead Souls was rightly called by the author a 'poem', for
it cannot be translated without losing much. In this it
resembles another profoundly national work, which sometimes the foreigner feels (wrongly) to have been over-rated,
Don Quixote. Each of them displays not only the national
scene but a way of thinking inseparable from the native
speech. Gogol, as he says at the end of his fifth chapter, is
interested in the 'home-grown, lively and adroit Russian
mind'—which had shown itself already in Krylov's fables.
Here it takes a larger opportunity, working not in a limited
genre but almost on epic scale.

Gogol's intention, as he told Pushkin in a letter of 1835,
had been 'to display at least from one side the whole of
Russia'. Thus *Dead Souls* no less than *Eugene Onegin*
could be described in Belinsky's phrase as 'an encyclopaedia
of Russian life'. The first part, published in 1842, Gogol
later called 'the porch to a palace, the vestibule of a grand
poem'. Some chapters of the second part, striving to undo
the havoc of the first, have survived and are much inferior;
the 'grand poem' itself, still incomplete, was destroyed by
its author in a fit of religious melancholia a few days before
he died. However, the first part is a beautifully balanced
whole, and has the straightness and force of great writing.
Excess was Gogol's natural mode and with him it wears the
authority of plain truth.

Gogol's whole aim is to generalize: the little provincial
town NN to which Chichikov goes on his peculiar mission
is exactly like all other provincial towns, just as the *brichka*
in which Chichikov travels can be categorized with
precision: it is a bachelor's vehicle, used by such people as
'retired lieutenant-colonels, staff-captains, landowners possessing about one hundred peasant souls, in a word, all
those who are called middling gentry'. Manilov's bailiff

has run the career of all other bailiffs, and now he behaves like the rest of them; Mme Korobochka is 'one of those good women, small proprietors, who weep at a bad harvest or loss and hold their heads slightly to one side'. The land-owners whom Chichikov visits—cloying Manilov, suspicious Korobochka, violent and mendacious Nozdryov, bear-like Sobakevich, hoarding Plyushkin—all have the finality of Jonsonian 'humours'; the town officials likewise, down to the public prosecutor who dies suddenly and has left behind him no memory except that of his bushy eyebrows. It is not surprising that Gogol's contemporaries saw his 'poem' as a measured indictment of all that offended them in Russian society. This, they felt, must be 'realism' (the term appears during the 1850's) of the most searching power. Gogol himself by his procedure seemed to underline this.

At the same time he sought for inclusiveness. This shows in the famous simile (Nabokov has discussed it in his spirited and very personal essay) of the light grey old uniforms of garrison soldiers, which the sky over NN at once put you in mind of: garrison soldiers are 'a peaceful body, by the way, but inclined not to be sober on Sundays'. Gogol's long-tailed similes all go to strengthen this sense of inclusiveness. Sobakevich's face from afar looks like a pumpkin, and that reminds Gogol of the light two-stringed balalaikas that are fashioned from pumpkins, and how exactly the village lad will play them, 'winking and whistling at the white-bosomed and white-necked maidens'. And as if the dense writing of the earlier chapters had not done its work, he sends Chichikov on a troika ride through vast representative tracts of Russia, where every village, every tavern or belfry or post, the vehicles on the road, the crows in the sky and the unbounded horizon, are all backed with a thousand like them, and compose Russia the unrelieved and unchanging.

Thus Gogol appeared to be, like Pushkin, another 'poet of actuality'. He may even have seen himself in this light. 'I have never created anything in my imagination and never had this faculty. I was only successful with what I had taken from reality, from data that were known to me.' As a child, he tells us, he had 'a passion for observing people'; and like Balzac—and perhaps even more like Dickens and Joyce— he is a hoarder of detail. He resembles his own Nozdryov, who in the course of fabricating a story was presented with 'such interesting details that he couldn't possibly refuse them'. Gogol is unable to resist telling us about Chichikov's travelling box, for example: 'The author is convinced that there are to be found readers curious enough even to wish for an account of the plan and inner arrangements of the box. Well then, why not satisfy them!' He complains in a famous passage at the beginning of Chapter 7 about the 'dreadful . . . mire of trivialities entangling our life', yet no man seems to have had a keener relish for trivialities. Gogol—or one side of him—could be claimed as an artist of the Flemish school (a term Pushkin applied half ironically to himself). What he does is to expand such catalogues of appearances as Pushkin gave in *Onegin* when he describes Tatyana's first sight of Moscow (VII, xxxviii) or the arrival of guests for her nameday (V, xxv–xxvii). So Belinsky felt no uneasiness in placing Gogol first for his power of 'representing in all its truth' the everyday life of Russia, its triviality, ugliness and monotony. When he speaks of a tendency stemming from Gogol he means the new realism to come: that determined exposure of social abuses for which Saltykov-Shchedrin became famous. Gogol found himself the critics' novelist. For them, in Cherny-shevsky's words, he 'stood at the head of those who repudiate what is evil and banal'.

About the banal little need be said after Nabokov's celebrated bravura-piece on 'poshlust',[3] that expressive word for the complacent and the trivial. Gogol was fas-cinated and horrified by the innumerable void gestures in life—especially those of bureaucrats. When Chichikov goes to the Chancellery the papers ratifying his purchase of mere names (the 'dead souls') are put through with much cere-mony. This was the shadow-dance of officialdom that Gogol detested. The next episode, where Chichikov the

'Kherson landowner' is fêted at a ball, continues the farce and widens the exposure. Here gestures and meaning have no possible point of contact. *Dead Souls* was so named to hint at a spiritual condition. Gogol has written the critique of pure vacancy.

His attention to the pettiness of provincial life led others to look at it with the same irony and impatience. What none could imitate was the peculiar 'laughter through tears' —the tragic sense imparted in terms of an absurd private fantasy. He delights, as I have said, in the blatantly average: Chichikov is realized on the first page by a bracketing technique: 'not handsome, but not bad looking, neither too stout nor too thin; it could not be said he was old, and yet he was not too young either'. Chichikov is strangely absent from life. He carries about his own environment: the *brichka*; Selifan his coachman; Petrushka his servant with the curious defining smell; and finally—it is part of his environment—the assumed ingratiating personality of 'Pavel Ivanovich', who charms by his obliging ordinariness. He is without ties; unmarried; nobody except himself knows his past (revealed only in the eleventh chapter). Yet he brings into the drab provincial world an illusion compelling in its vividness: the illusion that the dead souls— names on a paper given him for a few roubles—are alive and necessary; that they matter far more to him than the living. For what are the living? Numbered among them at the start was the public prosecutor, whose funeral Chichikov witnesses in the final chapter. All the town dignitaries and their wives are present, the dead burying the dead:

> opening the leather curtains [of his *brichka*] he sighed and uttered from his heart: 'See now, the public prose-cutor: he went on living, and then he died! . . . and if one examines the matter properly, it will be shown that all you had was bushy eyebrows.'

(XI)

Nothing else remains of that imposing and benevolent figure with its one eye perpetually winking, that indefatigable signer of documents and ready hand at whist. His death for the first time made him actual: 'Only then did they recognize with compassion that the departed had a soul, although in his modesty he had never displayed it' (X).

By contrast the peasants whom Sobakevich sold to Chichikov are not, as he insists, mere flies like people living today but real men. Everything is 'sound as a nut'; and Mikheyev his coachbuilder, Probka the carpenter, Maksim Telyatnikov the shoemaker still possess (for Sobakevich) their unique strength and dexterity. Chichikov in the hotel bedroom takes out Sobakevich's list of their names with particulars: 'All these details gave you a special kind of freshness: it seemed as though the peasants had been alive only yesterday.' So the rational mind puts it, but in the eyes of imagination, as Chichikov contemplates their names, they are still endowed with intense life. He reads over Plyushkin's list of runaway serfs, and can see them still wandering over the breadth of Russia: 'Abakum Fyrov! What of you, brother? In what parts do you wander? Did you get as far as the Volga, and did you make the free life your own, joining the barge-haulers?' (VII).

Gogol not only exposes but delights in 'the dangerous prevalence of the imagination'[4]. The first landlord whom Chichikov visits, Manilov, has on his estate a summer-house inscribed 'The Temple of Solitary Reflection'. To this pursuit Manilov has yielded up his whole being: nothing ever gets done at Manilov's house; illusions circulate there like paper money in a runaway inflation (his child has already become for him an ambassador, the Tsar hearing of Manilov's friendship with Chichikov will make them both generals). And Manilov gives the key to the character of those proprietors who will follow: solipsists all, to a greater or less degree. Yet Gogol views Manilov by no means simply. He satirizes the inefficiency, the complete alienation of Manilov from things as they are; but he enters joyfully into the dream, when Manilov

pondered the felicity of a life of friendship, how nice it

would be to live with his friend on the bank of some river, then across the river he began to construct a bridge, then an enormous house with such a lofty belvedere that from it you could see Moscow, and there drink tea of an evening in the open air and discuss various agreeable matters.

(II)

Each of the others, too, lives by his fantasy. Sometimes, as with Sobakevich, the fantasy succeeds in transforming the immediate surroundings: Sobakevich's squat house, with its bear-like furniture and portraits of hefty Greek patriots, is a dream solidified:

Chichikov once again glanced round the room and all that it contained—everything was solid, clumsy in the highest degree and had a strange affinity with the master of the house himself: in a corner of the drawing-room stood a paunchy walnut bureau on four most ungainly legs: an absolute bear. The table, armchairs, seats, everything had an oppressive and disturbing quality, in a word every object, every chair seemed to be saying: I too am Sobakevich! or, I too am very like Sobakevich!

(V)

Accordingly it is not difficult for Sobakevich to convince Chichikov that his dead peasants have the same solidity:

But indeed it's no dream! I am telling you what a man Mikheyev was, you cannot find such people: such a great machine, he couldn't get into the room; no, this is no dream!

(*Ib.*)

Similarly, Plyushkin amid his junk, Korobochka amid her old woman's fears, and Nozdryov amid his fertile and increasing lies, never escape from their own private fantasies. Korobochka, for example, is the kind of person from whom every proposition 'bounces off, as a rubber ball bounces off a wall'. Plyushkin has abdicated life altogether. The recollection of a boyhood friend produces on his 'wooden face' 'a sort of pale reflection of feeling', like the last glimpse of a drowning man that serves only to emphasize the desolation when the waters close over him. Nozdryov has become so thoroughly the victim of his own lies that he destroys his one moment of glory, piling invention upon wild invention until the officials who have turned to him in despair for information about Chichikov shrug their shoulders and walk away.

Finally, at the ball, the whole society of NN submits to the illusion of Chichikov as the 'Kherson landowner' and probably, at that moment, the most likeable man on earth. Gogol's attitude throughout the novel is obviously not one of plain condemnation; he does not deliberately set out to expose an odious regime or a deplorable way of life. Yet, while reading clearly enough the 'cold prose' of actuality, he weaves into it the arabesques of his own mind. This is less to show up the order of things than to supplant it.

So an entire society—the whole of Russia 'displayed at least from one side'—gives in to Chichikov (and he is, as Belinsky noted, no less a 'hero of his time' than Pechorin in Lermontov's book). Chichikov pays his visits to the élite of NN—governor, police chief, postmaster, the local proprietors—and then seeks out the last individually to make his peculiar treaty with each. The moment of bargaining has a macabre reality of its own. Whereas Chichikov, the general favourite, is created by rumour and afterwards destroyed by rumour (once the two 'agreeable ladies' have met together), and bears no meaningful relation whatsoever to the world of NN, Chichikov, the speculator trading in dead souls, entities no more solid than the 'Potemkin villages' with which her favourite once deluded Catherine II, comes fully alive in this act. Here he does exist for them, and gains the earnest attention given by those who feel that something of unsuspected value may be slipping between their fingers. At least they recognize Chichikov as the man who has a use for part of their property—a part they had hitherto neglected but which now acquires a money value, hence is significant. Chichikov's quest for dead souls revealed them as an 'interest'. Since all the excitement in NN centres upon this 'interest', the dead souls become, so to speak, the animating principle of the society. Each of the five proprietors has this secret in common with Chichikov. And in their private encounters with him they have exposed what they essentially are, so that here there exists a reality never acknowledged in the public talk and the celebrations that surround Chichikov in his glory. Without warning the glory leaves him. Chichikov, behind the curtains of his *brichka* contemplating the funeral procession, has become invisible once more, a nonentity for them all, just as they are remote for him, lost in thoughts of their own mortality; and finally their wives in the carriages are seen talking and gesticulating, but what they are saying can only be guessed. Chichikov no longer connects with them; so far as they are concerned, he has evaporated; and once again their activities have become the dance of death that they always were, before Chichikov's mission brought to them a few hours of vicarious life.

Russia (human society) exists for Gogol as a real landscape diversified by talk. Fields, forests, houses, even Manilov's summer-house, are all actually there, but it is talk that creates human society, and it is by words that men live and objects have character. Gogol is as eloquent a writer as Joyce, with the same trust in the almost magical properties of words; and like Joyce he tries out every form of jargon, the idiom of classes and occupations, all the vanity, the guile and insincerity latent in language.

Chichikov, when introducing his proposal to Sobakevich,

began very distantly, with a general reference to the whole Russian realm, and expressed himself in most laudatory terms about its extent, saying that even the ancient Roman monarchy itself was not so great, and foreigners rightly felt amazement . . . Sobakevich listened all the while with his head bowed . . . About his principal object Chichikov expressed himself most guardedly: he never called the souls 'dead' but merely 'non-existent'.

. . . 'You need dead souls?' asked Sobakevich quite simply, without the slightest surprise, as though they were talking of corn.

'Yes,' answered Chichikov, and again he softened the expression, adding 'non-existent ones' . . .

(V)

Everything is made possible by talk. At the celebration when Chichikov's papers have been signed,

> they argued, shouted, talked about everything, politics even the art of war, and they expounded free-thinking ideas for which at any other time they would have whipped their children. They settled there and then a multitude of extremely difficult questions. Chichikov had never felt in such a cheerful mood, he already imagined himself to be a real proprietor from Kherson, he spoke of various improvements: three-field agriculture, the happiness and beatitude of two souls, and he began to recite to Sobakevich Werther's epistle in verse to Charlotte . . .
>
> (VII)

Words help to fabricate the dreams by which Gogol's characters live. Either in their 'temples of solitary reflection', or carried away by the excitement of some public gathering, they escape from petty fact into spacious conjecture. And almost everyone is gifted with the same soaring fantasy. The two 'agreeable ladies' end easily enough by believing their own guesses; the officials are willing to think Chichikov may be Napoleon escaped from St Helena. Nozdryov merely abuses a faculty they all share. He creates with all the staggering particularity of Defoe, down to the name of the village priest who was to marry Chichikov on his elopement, the fee for the wedding . . . 'The details went so far that he began to name the drivers' (X).

Gogol's 'poem' ends with the flight of a troika which symbolizes Russian destiny. The passage is fine rhetoric;

and turning from Pushkin and Lermontov, so restrained in their prose, to this ebullience and headiness of Gogol, the reader becomes aware that a new tone has succeeded. The style of Pushkin, strict and unemotional, does not disappear; Turgenev, Goncharov, Tolstoy use and develop it. Gogol's demonstrative manner confirms the start of another tradition, that which leads eventually to Dostoevsky. There is a difference of temper here. Although Gogol owed much to Pushkin (including his subject for *Dead Souls*), he writes an exalted and lyrical Russian which promises something in the end alien to his master. With Gogol, whether he understood it or not, the sensibility of urban Russia, the mood of protest and denial, forced its way into prose fiction. Half the achievements to come in the great age of the Russian novel may be traced back to Pushkin. For the other half, strained and urgent and declamatory, Gogol was the prime mover.

PART TWO

PROSE PARAMOUNT

A note on the critics

FOR half a century after *Dead Souls* (1842) prose was to be the dominant mode. Despite a rare talent in Tyutchev (1803–1873), considerable charm in Fet (1820–1892) and Polonsky (1819–1898), and an impressive satirical and pathetic range in Nekrasov (1821–1877), poetry no longer held anything like an equality with prose. 'Don't ask the reason', Turgenev wrote in 1869, 'why there are no poets. There aren't any because there aren't any.'[1] And he predicted that they would surely come back, as indeed they did with the Symbolists. Meanwhile prose and the rational temper prevailed everywhere.

It was the same in Europe. 'The main effort', Arnold observed, 'for now many years, has been a critical effort.'[2] In Russia strong influences worked to convert everything into prose, and to put the novel, as Belinsky said, 'above all other kinds of poetry'. The age proliferated with ideas, and the continual debate between Slavophils and Westerners made Russia more idea-ridden perhaps than even the France of Proudhon and Comte. The fabric of belief and custom, which Peter the Great had already shaken, now came under violent strain. Democratic hopes, set back in Europe by the débâcle of 1848, lost none of their freshness for the majority of thinking Russians, who believed also in the inevitability of progress and the coming victory of science and reason.

The nineteenth century in Russia first assumed its character during the 1840's, when Vissarion Belinsky (1811–1848) made himself the schoolmaster of three generations. He was undoubtedly the most influential critic

of any country in an age that was to see many such, Sainte-
Beuve and Arnold among them. Belinsky had no literary
gifts, and wrote always against the clock. He expected no
subtlety from his readers, whom he lectured with far too much
paraphrase and quotation. Yet his own vision was remarkably keen and undistorted. Turgenev has left it on record
that Belinsky possessed an almost infallible judgement for
works of literature. He could recognize talent in his own
day and though sometimes he gave undue praise, as to
Dostoevsky's *Poor Folk* (1847), fashion never misled him,
and his comprehension of the main currents in Russian
literature made for an exceptional breadth and firmness.
Belinsky might almost be called a saint of criticism: vanity,
ambition or personal bias were completely alien to him.
Thus whatever he judged he judged purely; and though a
committed writer, always kept absolute truth as his touchstone. For him literature must serve generous ideals and
not fail in civic responsibility. In the famous letter to Gogol
he wrote:

> You for all I can see don't properly understand the
> Russian public. Its character depends on the state of
> Russian society in which fresh forces are active and
> struggling for expression, but weighed down by a heavy
> yoke they find no outlet and all they bring is despondency,
> anguish, indifference. Only in literature, despite the
> Tatar censorship, is there life and progress. That is why
> the name of writer has such honour with us, and why
> success in literature comes so easily even with slender
> talent. . . .

Belinsky saw to it that the novelist was taken seriously.
If Trollope could complain that his countrymen read
fiction

> as men eat pastry after dinner—not without some inward
> conviction that the taste is vain if not vicious,[3]

the Russian public learned from Belinsky to search for its
own identity in great novels as in great poems.

Unfortunately the critics who came after him did not often show the same literary tact. The most talented of them, N. A. Dobrolyubov (1836–1861), openly professed his aim as being

> to discuss the manifestations of life itself on the basis of a literary work.

This, of course, Belinsky, eagerly scanning the literary horizon for portents of social change, had done too. But whereas he always, I think, respected the work as literature, later critics such as D. I. Pisarev (1840–1868) responded more often to its tendency than to its intrinsic merit. Had Belinsky or even Dobrolyubov lived to review Turgenev's *Fathers and Children* (1862), they would not have blundered like the partisan critics who actually wrote on it. Too often an author was judged by his political sympathies, real or imputed. Hence the long neglect of Leskov, early dismissed as a reactionary. The critic began to use literature for his own ends. In this, strangely enough, both Tolstoy and Dostoevsky went a long way to meet him. The Russian novel ought, on all counts, to have suffered from the growing view of literature as instrumental, a means of 'infecting' people with religious and moral truth, of combating nihilism, or routing reaction. Eventually grave damage was done to it, and the publicist critics who had been largely responsible lost their hold for a short while in the twentieth century. They came back with the consolidation of Soviet power. Many sins can be charged to the civic school in criticism; it had a few virtues. It impoverished the sensibility of its readers, and by prescribing too insistently the one method of social realism, spread monotony and tedium. At the same time, above all in the hands of Belinsky, it gave literature a sense of direction, a marked social awareness. The novel particularly had to face public issues and to endure their relevance. Surrounded by vigilant critics, however narrow the kind of attention they brought to his work, a writer of fiction knew that he carried large responsibilities, both to the public and to himself.

4

Goncharov and the myth of Oblomov

KEATS in a letter once described what a Russian would recognize as *oblómovshchina*, the condition of Oblomov:

> This morning I am in a sort of temper indolent and supremely careless. . . . My passions are all asleep from my having slumbered till nearly eleven and weakened the animal fibre all over me to a delightful sensation about three degrees on this side of faintness—if I had teeth of pearl and the breath of lilies I should call it languor—but as I am I must call it laziness. In this state of effeminacy the fibres of the brain are relaxed in common with the rest of the body, and to such a happy degree that pleasure has no show of enticement and pain no unbearable frown. Neither Poetry, nor Ambition, nor Love have any alertness of countenance as they pass by me. . . .
>
> (To George and Georgiana Keats, Feb.–May 1819)

Oblomov, the poetic novel by Ivan Goncharov (1812–1891), celebrates this 'sort of temper'. As the hero, Ilya Ilyich Oblomov, contemplates the sun sinking in quietude he recognizes what he was born for: 'to express the possibility of an ideally tranquil side to human existence' (IV, ix). Keats a few lines further on in his letter says that 'Very few men have ever arrived at a complete disinterestedness of Mind'. But Oblomov, at least with regard to Olga and Stolz, is 'influenced by a pure desire for the benefit of others', which Keats found such a rare thing. Indolence had kept him unspoilt, eternally the child at Oblomovka.

Goncharov's novel (1849–59) began with 'The Dream

of Oblomov' which forms the climax in Part I, preceding
the arrival of Stolz. As Oblomov lies on his couch he
receives visitors from the outside world, and in their
persons social life, political ambition, journalism pass by
him and are lightly dismissed. ('How vainly men themselves
amaze . . .') When stung by the criticisms of his servant,
Zakhar, Oblomov turns for justification to the necessity
that has made him; it is revealed in a dream of the old
days at Oblomovka. A particular moment concentrates
the full meaning:

> Sultry noon; not a cloud in the sky. The sun stands
> motionless overhead and scorches the grass. The air has
> ceased to eddy and hangs without movement. No tree,
> no water is stirring; over village and field lies an inviol-
> able peace—everything seems to have died out. A human
> voice resounds a long way in the emptiness. At fifty
> yards you can hear how a beetle flies past and buzzes,
> and in the thick grass a snoring goes on, as though
> somebody has tumbled there and is sound asleep.
>
> (I, ix)

The boy is now free to explore the garden, the ramshackle
gallery and the ravine: 'he seemed alone in the whole
world'. This vision of still noonday heat (found also in
Tyutchev's poetry) dominates the book: Goncharov is a
contemplative writer, the poet of a sustained mood, who
'watches the last oozings hours by hours'. Perhaps his
whole novel can be reduced to a few charged images—this
of the noontide, the lilac that fades with Oblomov's love
for Olga and is planted on his grave, the calm setting sun.
The tranquillity principle, a divine stasis, has for its emblem
'sultry noon': over the love of Olga and Oblomov 'the hot
weather presides'—'until they think warm days will never
cease'. Goncharov's novel is the history of an hallucination
in which time appears immobilized: hence the prominence
of its static images, and its slow meditative course, and the
paucity of action.

'The Dream of Oblomov' irradiates the whole novel

much as the vision of Eden in Book 4 irradiates *Paradise Lost*. Indeed Goncharov might well have kept the title of this chapter for the entire work, which is altogether Oblomov-centred, describing the genesis, the interruption and the ultimate recovery of his dream. Stolz tries vainly to rouse him; Olga believes she can give Oblomov a future; but his dream is too strong for them. Heart and soul he belongs to the past. Oblomovka still waits for him like the old nurse, fallen asleep over her knitting, to whom he returns after peering down into the dreadful ravine. When he tells Stolz, early in Part 2, how it would be possible to live for ever happily on the manor, under a cloudless sky, it is a brighter version of Oblomovka that he presents. Stolz, hearing his condemnation of modern life, protests that he argues like an old-fashioned book. To visit Oblomov on his divan is a return 'to the birch grove where he had roamed as a boy' (II, ii). Thus Oblomov perpetuates lost innocence and a vanished order of things.

Goncharov gave his book a simple design. It presents a mild drama with prologue, two main acts and epilogue. The first part sets Oblomov in his surroundings at St Petersburg—the dressing-gown, the divan, the ill-kept study; it shows his dependence on Zakhar his servant, a close bond of habit that neither can forgo; it brings in various friends, one of whom is to scheme against him; it narrates Oblomov's dream, and concludes with the arrival of his boyhood companion and exact opposite, Andrey Stolz. Thus the full quality of Oblomov has been given; he is accounted for, placed and revealed by an accumulation of careful touches. The second part introduces Olga with whom Oblomov falls in love, vacillates, retreats and then hears from her that she will never desert him. The third part sees Oblomov installed at Pshenitsyna's house on the Vyborg side; he is cheated by his landlady's brother, gradually he fails Olga, and by the end she renounces him to the coffee-mill, the pies and the round twinkling elbows of Pshenitsyna. The fourth part describes as it were the post-humous life of Oblomov; he has succumbed to the maternal (and later wifely) care of Pshenitsyna; Stolz, now married to Olga, untangles Oblomov's debts; the principle of inertia descends to its close—early death by apoplexy. Oblomov has left a son by Pshenitsyna, Andrey, who will one day inherit an Oblomovka opened up by the railway; Stolz educates him, and also saves Zakhar from beggary. There has been just enough action to make a story. From the reality he knows (his own passiveness) Oblomov ventures into illusion (the prospect of a changed life with Olga), and after a little suffering settles for the reality, which overpowers him.

Goncharov was aiming to depict one character Oblomov, or better one attitude to life *oblómovshchina*. This he possessed fully: Oblomov is, like Don Quixote, a metaphysical notion that imposes itself on the known world, judging and overturning it; he is also, again like Don Quixote, held fast by actuality; Zakhar breaks into his dream, and in part shares it, as Sancho does with Don Quixote. And Zakhar is not hypothetical, a marvellous figment, but the Russian serf of a particular period:

> He belonged to two epochs, and they had both put their seal upon him. From the one he inherited a boundless devotion to the house of Oblomov, from the other and later a sophistication and corruption of morals.
>
> (I, vii)

Goncharov is the observant critic of manners, much like Turgenev; and by such precision in placing the servant he makes the master a social fact, representative of the declining gentry. (Oblomov owns and receives his income from three hundred serfs.) In the same way Stolz is accounted for as the son of an industrious German bailiff and a Russian mother. He, like Olga and Pshenitsyna, may owe his being to the plain logic of Oblomov's case, which demanded a man of action to balance the contemplative; a Tatyana to test Oblomov; a broad bosom to lull him asleep. But Goncharov's scheme no less than Pushkin's in *Onegin* works through observed fact. His

novel in the last resort is pure myth, Ilya Ilyich, as Renato
Poggioli has well said, bearing a fanciful relation to the
folk-hero, Ilya of Murom.[1] It starts as a poetic conception,
absolute idleness, but obeying the laws of the novel everything in it becomes relative, a matter of person, time and
place.

Therefore Dobrolyubov did no violence to one meaning
of the book in his decisive essay 'What Is *Oblómovshchina*?'
(1859). Before him Belinsky had taken the first novel by
Goncharov, *An Ordinary Story* (1847), at its face value, and
it had no other. Similarly, the third and last of Goncharov's novels, *The Precipice* (1869), is frankly a defence
of the old order, evoking all Goncharov had loved in his
childhood beside the Volga, maltreating a nihilist, and
making much of an autocratic old lady. From one point of
view even in *Oblomov* the author has written a social study,
though in the spirit of absolute truth and justice. Thus
Dobrolyubov could claim for *Oblomov* much the same as
Belinsky had claimed for *Dead Souls*: 'it reflects Russian
life and puts before us a live contemporary Russian type'.
'The word *oblómovshchina*', he insisted, 'serves as key to the
explanation of many phenomena in Russian life.' And
most skilfully he reveals in Oblomov's character the final,
degenerate form of traits present in other 'superfluous
men' and 'heroes of their time' as found in the fictions of
Pushkin, Lermontov, Herzen and Turgenev. He is able to
show a fixed pattern in the Russian novel whereby the hero
encounters a woman superior to himself and fails her, as
Onegin had Tatyana. Oblomovism becomes the name of a
contemporary disease—it results from the failure of nerve
on the part of an effete class. Dobrolyubov presses the case
very hard on moral grounds: Oblomov

> like Pechorin wants absolutely to *possess* a woman, to
> compel all kinds of sacrifices from her as evidence of her
> love. . . . He was not satisfied with Olga's consent, and—
> what do you think?—he began to try her . . .

Through his unsympathetic judgement Dobrolyubov seeks

to discredit the gentry of the kind Turgenev loved to portray, as incapable of action and unworthy of sharing in the new life (hence Olga's final break with Oblomov: her 'simplicity and clarity of mind' are the pledges for Dobrolyubov of something better than the existing order). Once Dobrolyubov had put the matter in this light, there was some excuse for reading *Oblomov* as an act of exposure, which Goncharov had performed in obedience to his nature as artist.

Dobrolyubov's view is, of course, one-sided. Like the novels of Turgenev, this work does bear the pressure of its own time: it was first conceived in the 1840's, a decade notable for social awareness; but it goes beyond nearly everything written by Turgenev in its profundity. What Turgenev has mostly to offer is the transcription of manners, which he does with a feeling accuracy. His art exhibits the surface; it lacks the intensity of myth. Goncharov, taking his time, discovered in *Oblomov* a master-theme that concentrated abilities perhaps inferior to Turgenev's, and gave them a unique chance. Just as *The Pilgrim's Progress* brought to a focus the whole of Bunyan's life, a success that could never be repeated, so *Oblomov* stands as the necessary act of Goncharov. In the one book he expressed the poetry of his situation. The other writings are prose.

Oblomov is a meditation at once ironic and sad on a way of life passing and soon to vanish. We have seen it in the second chapter of *Eugene Onegin* (the Larin family); it is there in the continuation of *Dead Souls* (Tentetnikov); Tolstoy was to look back at it in the Rostovs of *War and Peace*. For Goncharov it can persist through Oblomov's dreams. In his final rest at Pshenitsyna's, the past steals back into the mind of Ilya Ilyich:

'I simply can't thread this needle. Come, Masha, you have the sharper eyes.'

Lazily, mechanically, as though in a trance, he looked at the landlady's face, and from the depths of his memory there rose a familiar image seen by him somewhere. He tried to make out when and where he had heard this . . .

And he sees the big, dark drawing-room, lighted by a tallow candle, in his parents' house, and sitting at the round table his deceased mother and her guests; they sew in silence; his father paces in silence. Present and past have merged and become confused.

(IV, ix)

Oblomov himself seems to have escaped into the dream:

Ilya Ilyich was living as though in a golden frame of life, where as in a diorama only the usual phases of day and night and the seasons changed; other vicissitudes, especially those large contingencies which stir all the sediment, often bitter and troubled, from the depths of life, did not exist.

(*Ib.*)

He can realize his ideal only by renouncing all other ties and possibilities. Oblomov's quietude is almost a spiritual feat:

With the years agitation and remorse appeared less often, and he quietly and gradually settled into the simple broad coffin fashioned by his own hands out of the span remaining to him, like those venerable hermits who shun life and dig their own grave.

(*Ib.*)

Olga in her marriage with Stolz must endure the pains of maturity: she now sees what lies beyond their immediate happiness:

Leaning upon [Stolz] mechanically and slowly she walked down the alley, deep in a fixed silence. Fearfully she looked after her husband into the distance of life where, in his words, would come the time of 'trials', where 'sorrow and labour' were waiting.

(IV, viii)

This scene has its counterpart in the next chapter:

Here Ilya Ilyich walks slowly along the path, leaning

upon Vanya's shoulder. Vanya . . . can scarcely check his own vigorous, hasty steps to keep at Oblomov's pace. Ilya Ilyich has some difficulty in moving one leg—the result of his stroke.

(IV, ix)

No trials or labours await him: all he wants is to finish the walk and get back to fish soup. He has already prepared his peace.

Goncharov was in his own fashion, and no less than Belinsky, Tolstoy or Dostoevsky, an extremist. Against their incessant activity he places another extreme—that of inertia. They lacerate themselves in the struggle: he patiently holds his own. Tolstoy and Dostoevsky explore many kinds of experience that were beyond Goncharov; but he stuck to his single thought and developed it till the whole novel was saturated with the idea. He makes indolence a cosmic principle that enfolds all the petty traffic and hum of nature. So his novel takes on philosophical breadth, fullness and self-sufficiency. Like *Dead Souls* it should have been called a 'poem'. With the 'natural school' it never really belonged: all its abounding detail serves not to document a case but to substantiate a vision.

5

Turgenev in *Fathers and Children*

IVAN TURGENEV (1818–1883) was the kind of novelist the young Henry James wanted to be. He had grace and irony, he never lost his composure, he understood both Russia and Europe. James called him in a celebrated phrase 'the novelist's novelist'.[1] He was no less the European's European, who never shocked as Dostoevsky did with rabid Slavophil outpourings, never perplexed by a mystical faith in the Russian commune or Russian poverty. Turgenev believed in a more intelligible thing: the language itself, 'great, powerful, just and free'. He was the ideal ambassador of Russian letters in Paris; a man with whom George Eliot felt 'innumerable bonds of sympathy', as she did with Renan. It scarcely surprises that James should have included him in *French Poets and Novelists*.

Yet he had once stood at the centre of Russian life. Belinsky inspired him in the 1840's; he had been the intimate of Bakunin, and at another time of Tolstoy; he wrote for *The Contemporary* until Chernyshevsky and Dobrolyubov alienated him. His concern was always with Russia, and in the first place with the greatest evil in Russian life, serfdom. Even his long absences abroad did not make him a true cosmopolitan. James detected the 'Muscovite, home-loving note' that 'pervades his productions'; while at a distance, Turgenev kept watch on Russia. He seems to have felt responsible for Russian letters, encouraging new talent, and writing from his deathbed to persuade Tolstoy that he should return from dogma to literature. However 'Western' his manner may be, his loyalties are Russian.

Pushkin, always the master for Turgenev, taught him a

63

tone and a perspective. They belonged to the same class
(Turgenev had wealth besides rank); and they appreciated
the same things: a simplicity in elegance—the note of
Tatyana's drawing-room; independence and honesty; the
good sense of the practical Russian mind as they saw it;
in a word, the virtues of humanism. Neither showed any
real interest in religion. Scepticism is their strongest trait—
the humane scepticism of the French eighteenth century,
which consorts with an impulse to sympathize and seek
justice. Pushkin's range is much wider and his intellect
sturdier; irony in him might be called active, whereas in
Turgenev it tends to withdrawal, and is never quite proof
against a sentimental posture. Turgenev was more obviously dependent on Pushkin than, for instance, was
Tolstoy who also learned much from him. Yet he did more
than modify Pushkin for his own age. As Dobrolyubov
saw, he had a flair for noting the point of change and the
new forces in social relations. Here he was pupil both to
Pushkin and Belinsky. From Belinsky he learned to heighten
that historical sense which is everywhere present though
not always obtrusive in Pushkin's work. A novelist who
had conversed with Belinsky could not fail to look for the
least hint of innovation; social life was a developing
process.

Turgenev started out as a poet, though a negligible one.
In his last work, the *Senilia*, he returned to poetry—or at
least to prose poems. And like his friends Flaubert and
James he felt a poet's regard for language. (Many novelists
—Balzac, Dostoevsky, Lawrence—use it more as a con-
venience than a discipline.) Turgenev's ease and limpidity
and his beautiful cadences mark the high noon of Russian
prose, as it had been initiated by Pushkin and Lermontov.
Yet the harmony of Pushkin—that dynamic relation between
opposites in, for example, *The Bronze Horseman*—becomes
a lesser thing with Turgenev. His quality was described by
Dobrolyubov as 'gentleness and poetical moderation', by
James as a 'rare discretion'. For the modern reader
Turgenev is often too suave; too readily he falls into what

Hopkins would have called his 'Parnassian'. Even in 1893 Chekhov could no longer accept the once famous 'poetry' of Turgenev—the set-piece landscapes and the 'young ladies with their seductive shoulders.' This delicate sentimental side of Turgenev is now seen as limiting. His real strength lay in close observation. He was what James stated him to be: 'a story-teller who has taken notes', with a 'passion for distinctness'.[2]

Fathers and Children (1862) is the fourth of six major novels that followed *A Sportsman's Sketches* (1852). But whereas the last two, *Smoke* (1867) and *Virgin Soil* (1877), seem almost an epilogue, *Fathers and Children* brings to a conclusion the quest of the preceding novels for the 'new man' or 'hero of his own time'. In *Rudin* (1856), *A Nest of the Gentry* (1859) and *On the Eve* (1860) Turgenev advanced from the rhetoric of Rudin to true singleness of purpose in the Bulgarian patriot Insarov—'a man', as James observed, who 'stands up on his feet'.[3] Turgenev had taken the measure of idealists and others in the serf-owning class, and revealed the moral facts of their situation. All his male characters except the Bulgarian are ill-matched with his truth-loving and dauntless heroines (those Lizas and Elenas who Chekhov said were pythonessess rather than girls). In these novels Turgenev, following Pushkin in *Onegin*, confronts an intelligence formed by Western and radical ideas with 'a nest of the gentry'. For him too a young girl's instinctive response was to provide the touchstone. When Elena chooses Insarov and not the Russian artist or intellectual she performs—so Dobrolyubov implied—a symbolic act. 'In her is expressed that confused yearning for something, that almost unconscious but irresistible need for new life and new people. . . .'[4] Thus he put a direct political meaning into the fable, which Turgenev resented. 'My convictions', he wrote to a woman friend, 'have not changed since I was young, but I never concerned myself nor ever shall with politics.' However, his novels were written in a period when politics went deep into literature; and Dobrolyubov had some excuse for relating the book to its immediate context. In the novel that followed, *Fathers and Children*, Turgenev attempted the full-scale portrait of a Russian revolutionary, though some of the outline had to be left in shadows.

The novel is constructed around Bazarov—medical student, brutal positivist, radical. To elicit what he is Turgenev sends him to the small manor of Arkady his college friend; involves him there in a quarrel with Arkady's fastidious uncle; then in a love affair which humiliates him; in a final dispute with Arkady at the house of Bazarov's parents; and in the sudden catastrophe of death from typhus. The other people serve to bring Bazarov variously to the test; in death, the ultimate test, he reveals all the strength and bitterness of his nature. Properly speaking there are three *events* in the story: the first when Bazarov invades the tranquillity of Odintsova with his violent declaration; the second his duel with Pavel Petrovich (the uncle); and the the third his death agony. With Pavel Petrovich—and eventually with his nephew—the quarrel is ideological; and the duel over Fenichka merely carries on their dispute of the tenth chapter by other means. With Odintsova—a grand lady though once she had been poor—the quarrel is in part ideological, but mainly Bazarov protests against the despotism of sexual love. And in his quarrel with death he meets a reality still more insulting. So he has three problems: that of the outsider in a society which he judges effete; that of the lover in spite of himself who is rejected (and here he retains some dignity); and that of a young man murdered by fate, which he resists to his dying breath. The novel, though it describes the ordeal of Bazarov, is rightly called *Fathers and Children*: Turgenev presents through this ordeal a familiar conflict.

Many years later he wrote to Saltykov-Shchedrin about the 'enigma' of Bazarov:

> I can't very well make out how I described him. Here was—and please don't laugh—a kind of fate, something stronger than the author himself, and independent of

him. I do know one thing: I had no preconceived thought, no tendency . . .

(January 1876)

Bazarov he explained in 1862 came to him as

> a gloomy, wild, grand figure, half emerging from the soil powerful, enraged, honourable and yet doomed to destruction, because it stands as yet on the threshold of the future . . . I imagined a sort of strange pendant to Pugachov . . .[5]

There are moments when Bazarov (like Stavrogin in Dostoevsky's *Devils*) seems to derive from Gothic romance:

> Bazarov splayed out his long cruel fingers . . . Arkady turned and got ready, in play, to resist him . . . But his friend's face looked to him so ominous, and such a far from playful menace appeared in the wry sneer of his lips, and in the blazing eyes, that against his will he felt timid . . .

(xxi)

Bazarov is Satanic perhaps in his 'fathomless' pride. Arkady asks

> 'Have you a high opinion of yourself?'
> For a moment Bazarov was silent.
> 'When I meet the man who doesn't get out of the way for me,' he said deliberately, 'then I shall change my opinion about myself.'

(*Ib.*)

This pride sustains him in the last hours. Yet despite the Gothic affinities Bazarov has nothing to do with Cain. Nor was he forsaken in childhood. He suffers from no oppression, apart from the discouragement facing all able but poor young men in Russia. The only exceptional thing about Bazarov is that he belongs to the future.

Arkady's father and that liberal ghost his uncle, like Bazarov's own parents, are reconciled to the existing order; and that means to serfdom. Bazarov believes that his 'tendency'—the destructive principle—will have popular sentiment behind it: that you must 'clear a space' for others to build. The work of levelling must go on, and many things dear to Turgenev—the pieties and the pretences together—are flung down. In Arkady's father (with the symbolic lameness) he chose a peculiarly weak country gentleman; in the uncle a very ineffectual champion of the ideas current in Turgenev's own class; in Odintsova a *grande dame* apathetic almost beyond belief. So much for benevolence, liberalism and fashion: Bazarov wants no 'civilization' of that kind: he is what Arnold would have termed an 'acrid dissolvent'.[6]

Turgenev professed to share all Bazarov's views, except over art. (Bazarov holds it ridiculous for Arkady's father to play the cello, and wants him to read a textbook on materialism instead of Pushkin). But what Turgenev said afterwards as apologist—the novel was attacked from all sides—may even confuse what he affirms as author in the story itself. The insensibility, the churlish dogmatism and one might add the provincial arrogance of Bazarov—these annoy and they are surely meant to annoy. Herzen refused to accept them as more than adolescent defiance. But though Turgenev's 'nihilist' (a name that stuck) discomfits the reader, his bad manners are not meant to obscure his good cause. ('Of course he had to crush "the man with perfumed whiskers" and the rest! This is the triumph of democratic principle over aristocracy,' Turgenev explained.)[7] The author himself is facing a dilemma which comes to a head in *Virgin Soil*. There Nezhdanov recognizes that his poetry makes him a poor revolutionary, and commits suicide. Turgenev lets Bazarov expel Pushkin, and it is doubtful whether Pushkin comes back at all convincingly, when Arkady sits with Katya on a bench under the tall aspen. Turgenev was prepared to suppress his own doubts in the name of democracy. He respected that crude energy in Bazarov's nihilism.

His projection of Bazarov—the most original thing in *Fathers and Children*—yet differs strikingly from that of

Dostoevsky's nihilists. Turgenev, we know, always began
with

> the vision of some person, or persons, who hovered
> before him, soliciting him . . . He . . . saw them vividly,
> but then had to find for them the right relations, those
> that would most bring them out . . .[8]

First, the hint of a new 'type': in this case, a young provincial doctor met briefly and by chance. Then, having
noted the figure, to work out the situations and courses
that seemed likely for him. With Dostoevsky the character
experiences an idea which drives him along in a terrifying
dialectic. Turgenev had to confess, in the year he began
Fathers and Children: 'Whatever I write, the result is a
series of sketches'; not, as with Dostoevsky, scenes in a
necessary drama. Bazarov's death, though finely imagined,
has no reason unlike Kirillov's death, or Stavrogin's. Herzen
was probably right in thinking that Turgenev got rid of
Bazarov by typhus because he could settle with him in no
other way. In Turgenev's eyes this death 'put the last
touch' to a 'tragic figure', and yet, he added, 'the young
people find it fortuitous'. The 'young people' saw that
his natural pessimism (it could not be called here a tragic
sense) had cut short the story. 'Russia needs me . . . No,
clearly she doesn't.' So Bazarov speaks his own epitaph.
He has 'fallen under the wheel'. Not, like Anna Karenina,
because his way of life had become unbearable, but because
all is vanity, and the strength and pride of Bazarov mean
nothing to nature.

Fathers and Children falls short of greatness if the
standard is taken from Tolstoy or Dostoevsky. It has the
merit of complete honesty: Turgenev seems to have written
the story almost in spite of himself; and except perhaps for
the pious hopes in the conclusion he has checked sentiment
firmly throughout. This was the occasion for him to concentrate all his powers on a theme of peculiar interest: the
essential work for which his talents had been maturing. The
first of these is the ability to connect: Turgenev possesses

the entire scene and has placed it in history. He is expert in relations, whether between individuals—take for instance Arkady's indulgence and his father's mixed shame and relief when they discuss Fenichka—or between the individual and society at large. He notes a careless pronunciation whereby Pavel Petrovich in his dispute with Bazarov assumes the negligence of 'the quality' in Alexander's reign; he catches the old-fashioned pedantry and rustic rigmarole of Bazarov's father, as Scott had done with the Baron of Bradwardine; and he devotes to Bazarov's mother a careful paragraph (too long to quote in full) which makes her a part of history:

> Arina Vlasevna was the genuine Russian gentlewoman of an earlier time; she ought to have lived two hundred years ago, in the old Muscovite days. She was very devout and impressionable, she believed in all sorts of signs, auguries, spells and dreams . . . she believed that if on Easter day the candles at mass do not go out, the buckwheat will come on well, and that a mushroom will not grow once the eye of man has looked on it . . . she would not eat . . . water-melons because a carved water-melon recalls the head of John the Baptist . . . she read no book at all except for *Alexis, or the Cabin in the Forest* . . . she knew that in the world there are gentlefolk who have to give orders and the common people who have to obey them, and therefore didn't dislike timidity on their side, or bowing to the ground; but she was very gentle and mild with her subordinates, she never let a beggar go without giving him something, and she censured nobody though she was inclined to gossip. In youth she had been very charming, played the clavichord and could make herself more or less understood in French; but in the course of many years' travelling with her husband, whom she had married against her will, she grew ampler and forgot both music and the French language . . .
>
> (xx)

This kind of perception might not have been possible with-out the stanzas on Tatyana's mother in *Onegin*; but Turgenev can also net fish unknown to Pushkin, for example Kukshina the emancipated woman (who may have helped Henry James to visualize his Bostonian feminists):

> On the leather divan half reclined a lady, still young, fair-headed, a little dishevelled, in a silk dress not alto-gether clean, with heavy bracelets on her short arms and a lace kerchief upon her head. She rose from the divan and carelessly drawing on to her shoulders a glossy pelisse of yellowed ermine, she drawled:
> 'Hallo, Victor,' and pressed Sitnikov's hand.
> 'Bazarov, Kirsanov,' he announced abruptly, in imitation of Bazarov.
> 'Please be welcome,' answered Kukshina, and turning upon Bazarov her round eyes, between which her little snub nose looked red and orphaned, she added 'I know you' and pressed his hand too.
> Bazarov frowned. In the small and insignificant figure of the emancipated woman there was nothing ugly, and yet the expression of her face had an unpleasant effect on the beholder. It was difficult not to ask her: 'What's wrong, are you hungry? or bored? or frightened? Why are you all strung up?' She like Sitnikov was always on edge. She spoke and moved very unconstrainedly and at the same time awkwardly: it was clear she counted her-self a good-natured and simple being, and yet whatever she did you kept thinking she hadn't precisely meant to do that; everything with her was done, as children say, 'on purpose', and not simply and naturally.

(xiii)

And like Pushkin—like all novelists who concern themselves with 'the meaning of aspects'—Turgenev notes carefully her surroundings:

> The room in which they found themselves was more like

a working study than a drawing-room. Papers, letters, thick copies of Russian journals, mostly uncut, were scattered on dusty tables; everywhere was a white litter of cigarette ends.

Contrast with this Fenichka's sweet-smelling room with its lyre-backed chairs, the china egg hung from the halo on an ikon of Nicholas the Miracle-worker, and the caged siskin (viii); or the jumbled 'study' of old Bazarov (xx). These are all forms where a hare has lain.

Turgenev may be compared with Thackeray in his general attitudes: an early radicalism modified with the years; a certain hauteur; and a deep-seated pessimism. Both respond to the spectacle of this world, its brightness and variety, the grain on the social surface; they observe keenly and feel humanely. And both write with the same effortless grace and sensitivity to all the nuances of the spoken word. Turgenev is not free from sentimentality, though (unless in *Smoke*) he can hardly be accused of cynicism. The deep difference between them shows in Turgenev's superior moral courage. He never conceded anything to the public, but braved misunderstanding and even fury; his ideal of truthfulness puts him nearer to Mill than to Thackeray. Being a Russian, with a well-known Decembrist in the family, and the keenest consciences of the time among his personal friends, Turgenev learned a civic fortitude which did not issue in politics but in his practice as an artist. Liberalism was to become under the ridicule of Saltykov-Shchedrin an old, shabby word denoting the show but not the substance of democratic principle. But liberalism in the sense of free play for the humane, secular mind never had a more faithful adherent than Turgenev. He was in the 1850's what he had called Belinsky, 'the right man in the right place'. But after 1861, when liberal politics gave way to revolutionary, his place had gone.

6

Leskov and the righteous man

BELINSKY'S moral earnestness had behind it a long line
of village priests—his ancestors. The family of Nikolay
Leskov (1831–1895) for generations provided the village
priests of Leski in central Russia. Like Belinsky, Leskov
cared passionately for 'righteousness'; unlike Belinsky he
held that 'we need not good institutions but good people'.
His search for the righteous man (*právednik*) led him to the
minor clergy and the sectarians or Old Believers. He saw the
village priest as a link with the true Russian past, the world
of oral legend and popular art (Leskov wrote knowledge-
ably on the techniques of ikon-painting). All that was
national, singular and deep-rooted appealed strongly to
him. Six or seven years spent travelling on business through
remote tracts of Russia showed him popular life as few
among his contemporaries had seen it. Leskov prided
himself on knowing the people 'not from study but from
experience'.

He certainly knew their language in all its curious by-
ways and forgotten reaches. Leskov was a writer who loved
the pigments of language almost for their own sake.
Tolstoy once warned him that his faults of deliberate oddity
were too glaring: there was 'an exuberance of images,
colours, characteristic expressions, which intoxicates and
leads you astray'. But Leskov did not favour archaisms in
themselves. He was listening always for the tone of an
occupation or a surviving order: to catch the idiom of a
deacon, an Old Believer, a Tula craftsman or an Orel
merchant (*Lady Macbeth of Mtsensk*). In this he had no
rivals. The pure springs of popular Russian, sometimes the

lost springs, flow abundantly through his prose. A whole antiquated way of life is made manifest. He preserves a sight of traditional Russia as it appeared 'from the great house, from our own little hencoop of a manor, from the post station, and from the parsonage'.

His story of 1872, *Cathedral Folk* (as it has been called in the English translation), sees life from the parsonage. It deals with the decisive moment in the career of an arch-priest, Savely Tuberozov, who for some decades has looked after the principal church in Stargorod ('Oldtown') and its clergy. Savely is the noblest, the most convincing, of all Leskov's 'righteous men', modelled in part on his own grandfather. He is a witness to the truth after the style of Avvakum Petrov, the famous seventeenth-century recusant who endured hunger and cold and barbaric persecutions and still flooded the land with pamphlets and protests in the liveliest Russian idiom. Leskov opens his 'chronicle' with Savely's portrait, as bold and instinct with life as the ikon-painting by Andrey Rublyov of the Apostle Paul:

> Father Tuberozov was tall and portly, but still very hale and active. So too with his spiritual powers: at the first glance it was obvious that he had preserved all the fire of his heart and all the energy of youth. His head was extremely fine . . . Tuberozov's hair was thick as the mane of a great lion and white as the locks of Pheidias' Zeus . . . The brows of the reverend archpriest were quite black and moved in sharply broken Latin S's at the start of his nose which was pretty large and pretty broad. His eyes were tawny, large, bold, and clear. All his life they had not lost the capacity to quicken with the presence of reason; in them people close at hand could see the gleam of joyful rapture, and the mists of grief, and the tears of emotion: in them flashed too at times the fire of indig-nation and they cast sparks of rage—a rage not vain or captious or petty but the rage of a great man. Through these eyes looked the downright and honest soul of the

archpriest Savely, which he, in his firm Christian faith, believed should have everlasting life.

(I)

Tuberozov here is a righteous man in his panoply. We shall know him more intimately from the linen-bound notebook which he kept over thirty years, and from conversations he has with his submissive wife, and with the assistant priest, the deacon and a few other friends. There follow the portraits of his meek and bashful subordinate, Zakhary Benefaktov, harassed with a large family, and of the deacon Akhilla Desnitsyn (his 'strong right arm' is hinted at in his surname), a Cossack who behaves like Friar Tuck. All three are presented with the simplicity and vivid detail of folk-tale: Zakhary with 'feeble thin legs which are called strawy, and the whole of him seemed plaited from straw'; Akhilla's deep bass voice, that 'goes off like a gun'; Savely's lion mane and flashing eyes. And their houses belong to the world of folk-painting: Savely's in bright blue, 'with various coloured stars, squares and wooden pieces stuck on above each of its three windows'; Zakhary's 'a five-windowed, slightly crooked grey house . . . rather like a large aviary', alive with glimpses of little noses and forelocks behind the green panes; Akhilla's a Ukrainian cottage on the roof of which he maroons his housekeeper when she scolds him. Akhilla indeed is the traditional *bogatyr*, the strong man of folk-tale, but without his craft and good fortune.

In such a story there is the risk of quaintness. Leskov chose to write of 'candles burning out in an old parsonage'; he cherishes these people for their unworldliness and old-fashioned dignity. At one or two points in the novel, particularly when the golden-hearted dwarf comes to cheer and succour Savely, Leskov weakens; elsewhere his hand is firm. He keeps a distance through his control of language. Nearly always he invests himself in a speech disguise: either choosing a narrator, some experienced man with much local and unaccustomed lore whose idiom he can enter; or, as in this novel, reflecting the consciousness—and the vocabulary—of his protagonists. Leskov's vision begins in language. As Gorky said, he had not the plastic imagination of other novelists: his characters come alive through their speech, which is worked into the texture of the story-teller's own idiom. The Biblical and Church phrases here give the essence of a moral attitude that he admires for its simplicity. His whole relation with the subject is half teasing and half tender.

This may be seen from the affair of the walking sticks. A local magnate had presented each of the priests with a gold-topped cane, while the deacon got a silver one. But 'these sticks fell among the Stargorod clergy like the serpents of the Bible, which the Egyptian sorcerers cast before Pharaoh'. Akhilla began to invent scruples: was it right for him as a deacon to carry a stick, and why were the two given to the priests identical? When Savely goes into town taking Zakhary's stick with him, Akhilla begins to scent politics. Savely's return is followed by nearly a week's silence and when he does summon his brethren Akhilla burns with impatience to know what has been done. Even then it is some time before the sticks are produced. Both have the same device engraved on them: an all-seeing eye. Akhilla protests that there is no 'letterance' to distinguish the sticks. But Savely shows him that on the archpriest's stick are the words 'Aaron's rod blossomed' and on Zakhary's 'He gave into his hand a staff'. Finally Tuberozov decides to confiscate the deacon's stick, as not befitting his rank.

This 'example of the pettiness revealed in old age by the archpriest Savely' would be ludicrous but for the gravity of the actors, and especially the deep passion of Akhilla, who venerates Savely and is conscious of failing him too often. Already Leskov makes it clear that these three un-contemporary men are to be taken seriously. And the Savely who spells out his worth in the pages of the linen-bound notebook lives up to the initial portrait. Through the archaic words he expresses a spirit gentle but severe in its season; passionate for the truth; not to be overawed by prelate or official: the strain of Avvakum. Savely takes his own line with the Old Believers, and when their chapel has to be demolished he feels horror. The story was republished lately in the Soviet Union, no doubt because this priest challenges authority and writes in his notebook: 'I am not a philosopher but a citizen . . . Without activity I pine and suffer . . .' The entry is attributed to the year 1860. Father Savely responds in his own way to the civic ideal that stirred Chernyshevsky and Dobrolyubov.

Leskov was endlessly curious about Russian priests. His classic study *Details from Episcopal Life* investigates an order of men shielded in their personal life from the public eye. Innocent or crafty, gentle or imperious, sometimes the prisoners of their own grandeur, these Orthodox prelates meet his coolly discerning gaze. Leskov honoured Christian virtue where he could find it—as in the Metropolitan Philaret of Kiev. But others among these bishops were the merest politicians. Savely gets no support from his own father in God. As a righteous man he must sacrifice both his wife and his living in the cause of truth.

Father Savely's world has a good deal of absurdity in the background—as when the adversary of religion, Varnava the schoolteacher, tries to experiment on a skeleton which his mother steals from him to give it Christian burial. Savely himself never becomes ridiculous. From the beginning he is all of a piece, his first sermon foreshadowing his last. ('Afterwards however his lordship summoned me to him and, while approving my discourse in general, pointed out particularly that I should beware of relating my sermons directly to life, above all with regard to officials . . .') Father Savely is often indiscreet in a society where, as he notes, 'they are everywhere so scared by what is alive'. (Shchedrin could have written those words.) It is true that his unflinching candour wins him the regard of a despotic old lady who becomes his patroness, but she guesses that he must be lonely, in spite of a happy marriage: 'Every one of us who sees further in the family than his brother's

nose finds himself lonely even among his own folk.' In the
end Savely learns the full truth of her words:

> Tuberozov was very much resolved to do the deed
> which he had long meditated and had for a great while
> endeavoured, and of which he had told no one. And with
> whom could he take counsel? To whom could he tell what
> he had decided on? Could it be to the meek Zakhary, who
> 'is as though he were not'; or to the reckless Akhilla,
> who lives like a natural force, not knowing himself for
> what purpose and to what end he is applied; or to the
> officials or their ladies . . .? There was no one, not even
> his devoted Natalya Nikolaevna . . .
>
> The old man reflected. Thin streams of tobacco smoke,
> floating from under his grey moustaches and dispersing
> in the air, adorned with an amber necklace the rising
> sun; the hens flew off their perches and came out of the
> fowlhouse to shake themselves and to clean their feathers.
> Now on the bridge the shepherd blew his limewood pipe;
> along the bank empty pails on the women's shoulders
> told of water-carrying; the cows lowed, and the arch-
> priest's own servant, crossing her mouth as it yawned,
> drove the cow with a stick through the gates; the canary
> trills in its cage, and day is here in all its brightness.
>
> (III, viii)

Father Savely appeals to Leskov in part because of these
idyllic surroundings, but they do not make him the less
real.

Tuberozov faces a denunciation from the liberals of his
parish. He goes off on a visitation and is nearly killed in a
terrific storm. Where he had been resting a knight beset by
infidels was said to have prayed for deliverance. The light-
ning struck and in his place a spring of pure life-giving
water gushed out of the field. Tuberozov, also beset by
infidels, returns to his wife 'like an eagle that has renewed
its wings'. He preaches before the Stargorod officials a
sermon castigating their worldliness and lack of faith.
Martyrdom ensues: first the death of Savely's wife who has

followed him into confinement; then a year later, in solitude and disgrace, his own. All this Leskov narrates as a
zhitié, or saint's life, in tones of archaic simplicity.

The dwarf had once told Savely an 'old tale' which
comforted him. 'A wonderful thing is an old tale! . . . Oh,
how I should like to die in peace with my old tale' (II, v).
And he remembers a little wooden church that had been
cleared away to build a new stone one:

> . . . I missed the wooden church. A marvellous and
> bright new temple will they set up in Russia, and it will
> be bright and warm inside for our grandchildren at
> prayer, but it hurts to see how ruthlessly they cut down
> the old timbers!
>
> (II, v)

Leskov rejects the 'bright new temple', just as Dostoevsky
does the 'crystal palace' of socialism. Like Dostoevsky he
loses no opportunity to deride 'progress'. Varnava, the
scientifically minded teacher, is scared of his mother; the
excise officer's wife, who dirties hands and house as a sign of
free thought, resembles the absurd Kukshina in *Fathers and
Children*; and Termosesov, who acts the progressive, has
no sense of the past, no obligations, no principles:

> He seemed to have decided once and for all that
> conscience, honour, love and in general all the so-called
> elevated feelings were rubbish, muck, nonsense invented
> by philosophers, men of letters, and other crazy fantasts.
> He did not deny—that would have been too contro-
> versial—he merely knew that there was no such thing and
> therefore it wasn't worth dwelling upon.
>
> (III, xvi)

Termosesov is modernity: the cynical opponent of the 'old
tale' and the ancient virtues as found in Savely and his
colleagues, and also in the dwarfs, brother and sister.
This unlikely pair anticipate Fomushka and Fimushka in
Turgenev's *Virgin Soil*; and they are equally boring. In
return Leskov may have recalled Bazarov's mother when

he came to depict the wife of his archpriest. 'Where save in holy Russia can such wives be?' asks Savely. 'Such women are now becoming extinct', Turgenev had commented on Arina Vlasevna. 'God knows whether one should be glad of it.'

> In her strictness and frugality the archpriest's wife all the while she was with her husband in his banishment did without a servant and took upon herself labours which she was unaccustomed to and had no strength for. On coming down to the last 25-rouble note in her purse she was scared that they would soon have not a farthing left, and she resolved to ask her landlord the gendarme to delay their rent until pardon should arrive. The gendarme agreed, and Natalya Nikolaevna, carefully hiding all this from her husband, sought by every means to requite the landlord: she dug potatoes with his woman, chopped cabbage and took her own washing down to the river.
>
> (IV, xii)

Leskov cherishes Natalya Nikolaevna, with her tremulous devotion to the archpriest. Sometimes, as in the account of their ritual on bidding each other good night, or in that much earlier episode of the unseen string twitching Savely's handkerchief to distract him from writing, sentimentality almost creeps in. But the moral vigour of Savely himself and his wife's practical virtues prevent too hasty a dismissal. Russian writers have always responded to this kind of goodness without embarrassing or cloying the reader. This naïveté of Russian feeling is protected by humour—that 'slyness' which Pushkin had noted in the national character. It is further backed by a moral realism: after all, neither Savely's wife nor Bazarov's mother has a Dickensian immunity from the common lot.

Cathedral Folk might easily have become sentimental— a 'reactionary' book hallowing the fictitious past. However crude Leskov's first intention—to glorify the Orthodox Church as a bulwark against Poles and nihilists—Father Savely is no party to the plot. He belongs to literature not propaganda. And indeed Leskov came to doubt the excellence of the Orthodox Church; gave up baiting the nihilists; and searched now for the righteous man among those Old Believers whom Savely had been so reluctant to put down. The stern piety of Savely has little to do with established religion; he takes his place among those independent seekers of truth who do honour to Russian life and literature. Twenty years later Leskov replied to a critic who had reviewed his whole achievement:

> If I had written about myself I should have called the essay not 'A Sick Talent' but 'A Difficult Growth'. Aristocratic tendencies, church devoutness, narrow nationalism and loyalty to the State, the glory of one's country etc. Amid all this I grew up, and all of this often repelled me, but . . . I could not see where truth was.[1]

With the years, meeting 'the splendid people of the liberation period', he grew more radical. Some later pieces have a satirical force not unlike Saltykov-Shchedrin's. Leskov recognized that he had made mistakes and had not always been just. But his 'difficult growth' would not have been possible without that firmness of character which he projected in Tuberozov.

Compared with the Russian novelists of European fame Leskov has his limitations. He might almost be called the last medieval writer of Russia: a tale like *The Robbery* (1887) would have suited the genius of Chaucer. An Orel merchant looks back to the day when he and a solid uncle from Elets attacked on the ice and then robbed a deacon. The uncle had been entrusted by his fellow-citizens to find the most powerful-voiced deacon available for their church; this was the winning candidate. On the way home from the audition in an hotel, the uncle and nephew became scared, thought the nephew's watch had been stolen, and overtook the supposed thief whom they deprived of his watch and then beat up 'both in Elets fashion and in Orel fashion'. Leskov's characters—the homekeeping boy ruled by his mother, the pious merchants and the two contesting deacons—live in a world hardly touched by the nineteenth century. Again his fable *The Left-handed Craftsman* (1881), about the ingenious Tula locksmiths, Tsar Alexander and Platov the Cossack hero of 1812, is presented as pure folktale. Leskov knew in its fulness a Russia of stonemasons who carry their priceless ikons everywhere with them on a donkey (*The Sealed Angel*, 1873); of horsecopers turned monks (*The Enchanted Wanderer*, 1873); of vanishing trades and backward communities. Through his experience and through his marvellous ear for the spoken language he had access to popular life on the roads, in forgotten towns, in the slowly expiring medieval past. Those years of wandering with his English uncle Scott, a rich nobleman's factor, stamped Leskov as a writer of unusual knowledge. Gorky learned much from him, and the whole tradition of curious vernacular prose that includes Remizov, Zamyatin and Pilnyak had its origins with Leskov.

7

Tolstoy: art and conscience
(Anna Karenina)

TOLSTOY (1828–1910) was a poet who disbelieved in nearly
all poetry—the iconoclast of his own work. He combined a
spontaneity that seemed nature's own with a passion for
rectitude and the readiness to pluck out his eye if it offended.
Perhaps in such plasticity and such rigour he manifested
the two poles of the Russian temperament. This, as Gogol
and Lermontov complained and as Dostoevsky boasted,
can so easily take the colour of its surroundings. Also, as
we know from observation of Rakhmetov in Chernyshevsky's novel *What Is To Be Done?*, and of Nechaev in history,[1]
it can submit to a more than Hebrew severity, a more than
Spanish asceticism. The greatest writers admit both sides
of the debate in their own day: thus Pushkin is at once
radical and conservative, Tolstoy child of nature and jealous
moralist, Dostoevsky believer and infidel. Whereas Pushkin
harmonized what was dissonant, and Dostoevsky bore with
dissonance as the condition of life, Tolstoy wanted to
reduce everything to plainsong. He accepted poverty,
chastity and obedience as the rule for his imagination, but
only after a long struggle, and with constant relapses.

Tolstoy's earliest work—the more or less autobiographical sketches in *Childhood, Boyhood* and *Youth* (1852–
7)—at once revealed his gift of innocence. Sometimes
termed naïveté, sometimes the capacity to re-enter childhood, it is a grace to be found also in Oblomov. This
immediacy lies within the grasp of Pushkin and Lermontov;
but in Tolstoy it becomes his guiding light. He never lost
the capacity for wonder, for the Adamic vision such as we

find in Whitman and Thoreau. The genius of Tolstoy, despite its magnificent range, is simple. He desired wholeness above everything, and he began with sureties. His first inspiration was childhood: his original manner that of the purest writers in prose from his own background, Pushkin and Lermontov. The latter also in two poems, *Borodino* and the description of a skirmish at Valerik, gave him a clue for the *Sevastopol Sketches* (1855–6).

As he is simple, so he writes also, even at the plenitude of his powers, an old-fashioned novel. This becomes clear if we compare him with Dostoevsky. *War and Peace* (1866–9) belongs to a different spiritual generation from *Crime and Punishment* (1866), though they are so close in actual date. Something of *War and Peace* on a miniature scale appears, as we know, in Pushkin's unfinished story *Roslavlev* (1831). The Tolstoy who wrote his great epic of the war with Napoleon looked back because he disliked the present. *War and Peace* is a grand valediction to the heyday of the Russian nobility, and especially of that Muscovite rural section glorified in the Rostov family. It is also a pause for Tolstoy to assess not only the past of his kindred but his own experience hitherto. *War and Peace* might be called an apology for his house and himself, and it defends the ancient hospitality, the blunt old ways, the generous impulse and strong patriotic feelings of such men as Count Ilya Rostov against all their modern detractors. Kutuzov the wise laggard appears as a real man; whereas Speransky the academic reformer has no touch with the living world, thus anticipating Alexey Alexandrovich Karenin. In one aspect the book is concerned with spontaneity as against the fixed will.

Though often regarded as a lesser thing—domestic instead of national, his *Odyssey* after the *Iliad*—Tolstoy's main work of the 1870's, *Anna Karenina*, probably goes deeper and embodies even more thought than the noble expanse of *War and Peace*. And in *Anna Karenina* the earlier Tolstoy, master of the serene vision, lingers on, making room also for the angular and fierce Tolstoy of *Resurrection* (1899).

At no other point of his career do so many issues come to
a head as in this novel. The 'seventies form a peak decade
of Russian writing, with not only *Anna Karenina* but also
The Brothers Karamazov. It was a time of very intense
thought, of rapid social change, and of new political
activity which included 'going to the people' and the
terrorist plots leading to the assassination of Alexander II
in 1881. *Anna Karenina* is more of a novel than *War and
Peace* in so far as it has more in common with George
Eliot's *Middlemarch* (1872) than with the *Iliad* or Shakespeare's history plays, where we have to find the analogues
for *War and Peace*. As such it belongs more intimately to
the age than did *War and Peace*: Tolstoy brings into it the
crisis of Russia in the 'seventies, when—in the words Lenin
was so fond of quoting—'everything had been overturned
and was only beginning to settle down' (III, xxvi). All the
issues that were then troubling Russian minds come into
the book: the agricultural question, the 'woman question',
the problem of relation between the sexes and the right to
divorce, the peasant problem, the new liberalizing institutions in the countryside (the *Zemstvo*), Slavophil aspira-
tions, the Balkan wars of 1877 and 1878, science and
religion, nihilism and traditional piety. Tolstoy no less
than Saltykov-Shchedrin or Dostoevsky opened his pages
to the topics of the hour, and argued them passionately in
season and out. Russian writing in the third quarter of the
nineteenth century is frankly tendentious. This was the age
which admitted no poet except the 'civic' Nekrasov to
equality with the great novelists. Tolstoy and Dostoevsky
had to move through the element of controversy without
drowning in it. Both manage to argue their way into a larger
truth. The issues of the hour are taken into the keeping of
a timeless imagination.

Anna Karenina continues the debate of *War and Peace*,
setting spontaneity against the intellect and unyielding will;
rural sense, neighbourhood with the peasants and domestic
stability against the false civilization of St Petersburg. This
is one clear line of division that runs through the book,

but spontaneity itself, in the passion of Vronsky and Anna, and the irresponsible pursuit of pleasure by Stiva, now reveals a destructive power that was not hinted at in *War and Peace*. Whereas before Tolstoy had written from certitude, in this novel he brings up the formidable battery of scepticism which was to lay waste the natural man in him. *War and Peace* is almost a treatise on Russian patriotism: where in 1812 it was truly to be found, what virtues supported it, how it proved more resourceful because morally stronger than the *gloire* of the French invaders. Though saying much about war as an experience in itself, *War and Peace* keeps principally to this polemic design: it vindicates gentry and people, the Russian patriarchal past, the Moscow which made every true Russian heart beat more quickly. *Anna Karenina* sets out on the same bold course, but proves a more complicated novel. Tolstoy submits to a more rigorous questioning from his conscience as the book proceeds. Like *War and Peace* it was recast more than once.[2] In its final form *Anna Karenina* was a far richer work than at first planned, and a different one.

Originally *Anna Karenina* was to have been the story of a lost woman who deceives her elderly, kind husband. From the words of Pushkin's fragment (it has been mentioned in Chapter 1):[3]

> The guests had driven out to the summer villa of the countess . . .

Tolstoy took his cue for the opening of *Anna Karenina* in its first draft:

> The guests after the opera drove out to young Princess Vrassky's,

and the situation in what later became the sixth chapter of Part 2 closely resembles that sketched by Pushkin. Tolstoy, however, has altered the moral sense: not only is the woman indiscreet, she is wholly without shame. And as Tolstoy worked over his material he made the husband reflect that an evil spirit had taken hold of his wife whom he cannot recognize. But although the light is beginning to fall differently here, it was important that Tolstoy should have met with these fragments. When writing his stories for peasant children (such as *The Prisoner in the Caucasus*, 1872) he had been looking for an extreme purity of outline. And this rather surprisingly he found in Pushkin, a writer from his own class.[4] In rediscovering Pushkin for himself Tolstoy was confirmed in the attitudes and tones that belonged to the aristocratic line in Russian literature. And this probably kept *Anna Karenina* well within that tradition, so that it is, no less than *War and Peace*, a 'gentry novel'.

In course of time *Anna Karenina* grew and altered. The protagonists themselves—now named Anna, Alexey Alexandrovich Karenin and Alexey Vronsky—became the people we know. A gradual shift of emphasis undid Tolstoy's first plan. Anna retains something of her original wildness, but is less a woman possessed by the devil than a woman whose spontaneous vitality takes her outside the moral law.[5] Vronsky is groomed, given more presence and charm than in the original drafts, though he remains a 'social being', to use Lawrence's term: a man who has no genuine moral centre but lives by an elaborate code of male conventions. These enable him to be ruthless towards Kitty, and yet patient and honourable with Anna in the last stages when they are antagonized. Most important of all Karenin is recast as the cerebral creature (Greek *karēnon*, the head), a bureaucrat wedded to his portfolio. Anna might be described as a Muscovite by nature who has strayed into St Petersburg. If she offends against the moral law, as Tolstoy firmly believes, her affront to St Petersburg society becomes a virtue. She is thus reprobate and martyr: a fine spirit driven to wrong courses, and brought down by the howling pack. Tolstoy refuses to let humanity judge Anna: 'Vengeance is mine; I will repay, saith the Lord' (Romans xii, 19). The tragic sense is thus generated: Anna has done wrong (the treatment of her son, Seryozha, cannot be put aside), yet the impulse to leave Karenin, with his narrow, pedantic and cold nature, even though she is ruined thereby, makes her adultery seem like recovered innocence. This, of course, it is far from being. Tolstoy spares no evidence of her increasing misery and exasperation as she comes to realize that her new life, equally with her old, and yet more disastrously, is a lie. However, as Dostoevsky knew, passionate wrong is at least a kind of seeking. The very proportions of Anna's nature, her abounding verve, and the generosity that Arnold noted,[6] doom her to tragedy in the shallow world of Karenin.

Anna's guilt, and it may be her endowment with unmoral 'quickness' in the Laurentian sense, shuts her out from what Tolstoy represents as the 'real world', that in which Levin and Kitty move. This pair were latecomers into the design, but as the novel progressed Tolstoy used them to illustrate the 'possible other case', an attachment ironically out of Anna's reach. With Levin and Kitty also stands Dolly, the wife maltreated by Anna's brother. She is eager in her sympathy and gratitude to justify Anna's rebellion, yet on actually seeing the establishment of Anna and Vronsky she at once guesses that Anna lacks maternal feeling. Tolstoy wrote his novel in defence of the family, an idea that now absorbed him as that of the people had in *War and Peace*. Though he may exult in the life-asserting spontaneity of Anna, he fears her as a destroyer of 'family happiness'.

Yet Levin is not wholly at ease in 'family happiness'; he has a sore mind that constantly frets him. Levin, we know, represents Tolstoy to the extent of sharing some of his actual experiences (the telepathic test that leads to a proposal of marriage; the muddle over a shirt on his wedding day; the death of his brother Nikolay). And, like Tolstoy, much as he may pine for the tranquil routine of an earlier day (as shown in old Prince Shcherbatsky), Levin has been infected with the curiosity and conscience of the nineteenth century. His family home

was all the world for Levin. This was the world in which had lived and died his father and mother. They had lived the life that seemed to Levin the ideal of every perfection and that he hoped to renew with his own wife, his own family.

. . . Love for a woman he not only could not imagine without marriage, but first he imagined the family and then the woman who would give him the family.

(I, xxvii)

Yet the Levin who feels like this as he caresses the dog and half listens to the chatter of his old housekeeper is at the same time studying Tyndall. The nineteenth century will allow him no peace. Kitty has the instinctive faith of women and of the peasants in general, and Levin may escape from the useless talk of his half-brother the distinguished thinker to mow in deep mindless communion with the peasants; he may find salvation from oppressive thoughts of death when a peasant lets fall a casual word or two about 'living for one's own soul', 'according to the truth, in God's way'. However, as Dostoevsky observed, there can be no lasting rest for Levin who will rend his new-found peace on a snag before long. Tolstoy's own gathering moral and religious crisis not only makes itself felt everywhere in the second half of *Anna Karenina*; also it spoils the intended balance and contrast between Anna's career and Levin's. Anna in the headlong pursuit of personal happiness at the cost of home and family has destroyed herself; Levin, no less intent on personal happiness, which he seeks through home and family, is near destroying himself too. The ideal of rooted life is within his grasp, yet he cannot believe, or if he does believe after hearing the peasant it is temporarily and provisionally. Levin understands that faith cannot be made accountable to reason; but Tolstoy was to spend the next thirty years of his life trying to rationalize faith.

The argument in *Anna Karenina* centres around the disputatious Levin, who is as obstinate as any Starodum (or Oldwit) in eighteenth-century comedy. Levin cannot make sense out of his brother's theories; he distrusts the liberals and the would-be deliverers of the oppressed Slavs; he rejects the nihilism and revolutionary pathos of Nikolay, the brother whose death shakes so profoundly his confidence in the purpose of living. He argues even more with himself than with others. At one moment, lying on the haystack, he resolves to give up everything and marry a village girl.

> The simplicity, purity and rightness of such a life he felt clearly and was convinced that there he would find the satisfaction, peace and dignity the lack of which he so painfully felt.

Then he begins to consider ways and means, and is baffled.

> 'Anyway, I have not slept all night, and I can't give myself a clear answer,' he told himself. 'I'll clear it up later. One thing is sure, that this night has settled my fate. All my former dreams about family life were nonsense, not the real thing,' he told himself. 'All this is a great deal simpler and better.'
>
> 'How beautiful!' he reflected, looking at a strange mother-of-pearl shell of white fleecy clouds, which had halted right above his head in the middle of the sky. 'How delightful everything is on this delightful night! And when did this shell have time to form? Not long since I looked at the sky, and there was nothing there—only two white streaks. Yes, just so unnoticeably have changed my views upon life.'

(III, xii)

In a moment or two Kitty's carriage will pass by, and Levin's present thoughts be dissipated. When he next looks up, the cloud pattern will have broken.

The passage is, of course, celebrated, and nothing reveals more strikingly the other side of Tolstoy's intelligence— his marvellous apprehension of change and fluidity that dissolves every rigid argument. In the 1850's Chernyshevsky singled out as Tolstoy's greatest quality the insight with which he traced the 'dialectic of the soul', its 'interior monologue' (Chernyshevsky's own terms).[7] The dialectic does not reveal itself dramatically, as is the case with

Dostoevsky. It happens in moments of solitude, when
Prince Andrey lies on the field of Austerlitz, or the young
officer in *The Cossacks* (1852–62) is driving alone through
the night, or Levin walks silently down the roadway at dawn
as the bells on Kitty's carriage grow fainter ahead of him.

This delicacy of notation he shares with the poets—notably
Tyutchev, and his own friend, the disciple of Tyutchev, Fet.
Recently Eichenbaum demonstrated the link between their
sense of a living presence in nature and Tolstoy's.[8] From
Tyutchev he also gained a deeper understanding of the havoc
in passion, especially from the famous poem that begins

> How we do murder in our love!

(Tyutchev's cycle of poems on his tragic passion for Deniseva
made their appeal not only to Tolstoy but to Dostoevsky.)
The background to *Anna Karenina* is partly to be sought in
Tyutchev and Fet, partly in Schopenhauer. The full experience of the novel comes through as profoundly poetic.
All the argument stays on the surface: what moves the
imagination as in few other novels is the play of immediate
feeling, the effortless participation in every movement that
goes on behind the will and at the deepest levels of consciousness.

It is now fairly well known that Arnold (and Henry
James) were wrong in supposing *Anna Karenina* to be
virtually without plan. ('But the truth is we are not to take
Anna Karénine as a work of art; we are to take it as a piece
of life. . . . The author has not invented and combined it,
he has seen it. . . .')[9] The novel has an extremely rich
organization, more and more of which comes into view with
fresh readings. It works through contrast and correspondence; and Tolstoy had reason to pride himself on its
structure. There is the obvious main contrast between
Anna's world and Levin's, and the values implicit in each:
the St Petersburg setting and the Moscow setting; on the
one hand, heartless convention, on the other, heart-
warming simplicity. Anna's life, as we see it, is all an affair
of railway stations, of restless journeying and of fake

domesticity. Levin belongs to the country and to the old house of his parents. For Anna, happiness must be sought in passion; for Levin, in marriage. This simple contrast sets up the two poles of the story, each gathering its attendant themes and symbols. The aim shared by all the serious people in the book—by Anna and Levin, for instance; by Vronsky when he thinks of Anna's plight; by Kitty and Varenka—is 'peace and dignity'; and these words ring out clearly at moments of crisis in the book. Peace and dignity must take account of the experiences that transcend life— that is, of birth and death. Anna is directed towards death; Levin is redirected by his awareness of death. The birth of her daughter means nothing to Anna; the birth of his son is a secure joy to Levin who has just lost his brother and begun to doubt the purpose of life.

The story is blocked out in contrasting episodes, as it moves from one capital to the other, from town to country, from Russia to Italy. Through the multitude of incidents a deep underlying rhythm can be discerned. Thus in the opening book the lives of Dolly and Stiva, of Anna, of Vronsky and of Levin are all in their different ways disturbed. By the end of this prelude to the main action all seem to have settled down again in their old routines. Dolly is once more mildly bantering in her treatment of Stiva; Anna believes she has now fallen back comfortably and assuredly into the familiar life of her husband's circle; Vronsky resumes the regimental round like a pair of old slippers; Levin accepts his dog and the farmer's day. But all these returns are illusory; the new courses drive each of them on—Anna to her ultimate suicide, Vronsky to the Balkan wars, Dolly to further ignominies at the hands of her husband, Levin to happiness through marriage and then to a profounder disturbance that almost destroys that happiness. This rhythm has the look of destiny, at any rate in the lives of Anna and Vronsky, and of Levin and Kitty. From the beginning Kitty knows that she can find peace with Levin: that with him all will be open and natural. Anna's affair with Vronsky is dominated by the railway that has made possible their love, and will eventually separate them for ever. The declaration by Vronsky in the storm at a wayside station realizes a moment of tragic terror:

> And just then as though having overcome an obstacle the wind scattered the snow from the carriage roofs, shook some broken-off iron sheet, and at the front the deep whistle of the engine sounded wailfully and gloomily. All the horror of the blizzard seemed to her more beautiful now.
>
> (I, xxx)

This is the blizzard of destructive passion that blows through Blok's verse; it has the same note of finality. Anna is a free agent only inside the terms of her fate as Tolstoy has decreed them.

Much could be said about Tolstoy's attitude to Anna, and one might use against him some words he wrote on the heroine of Maupassant's *Une Vie*:

> You feel that the author loves this woman ... And the questions 'Why, for what purpose should this beautiful creature be destroyed? Must it really be so?' arise of themselves in the reader and make him reflect on the sense and purpose of human life.
>
> (1894)

Anna has been trapped by him in a false position through her marriage with Karenin—a *donnée* of the story that should not go unchallenged. Tolstoy refuses to have her judged by the mob of gentlefolk who sin with ease, yet implicitly he does judge her himself. There is an unavowed dread of Anna's magnetism in Tolstoy, and also a social bias which, by putting her in St Petersburg, can allow her no more worthy lover than the conventional Vronsky. Yet however dogmatic Tolstoy was by intention, he could not stay simply on the moral plane. The events move irresistibly into the realm of tragedy: Vengeance is mine; I will repay, saith the Lord. *Anna Karenina* became a much more impressive work than the later *Resurrection* because the heroine's appeal for Tolstoy refused to let him make her story into a treatise. Arnold was essentially right when he said of the novel: 'A piece of life it is.' There can be no short cuts in life: Tolstoy does not attempt them in *Anna Karenina*.

The novel form as used by Tolstoy (and for that matter by Dostoevsky) comes to have the scope and intensity of great poetry. It draws upon the experience that poets like Pushkin and Tyutchev had ordered; and it responds to the complexities of the age in the same manner as Shakespearian drama or Pushkinian verse-tale. Viewed from a certain distance, where the structure is most apparent, all three kinds of literature seem to achieve the same ends and to use the same comprehensive gestures; and while this is true at a distance, even close inspection has to admit such novels as a form of extended poetry. They are, one might concede, the poetry of large design which survives in a culture distrustful of poetry. Tolstoy and Dostoevsky rival Pushkin in completeness of response to the age. Pushkin's circumstances allowed for a formal perfection, an assurance and a simplicity that have never been possible to later generations. The world in which Tolstoy and Dostoevsky contended each for his own ultimate and exclusive vision shares so many more features with our own than does Pushkin's, that we accept more grudgingly the poet who stands behind both these novelists, the first major presence in Russian literature. At this level there can be no competition: each did the most that was possible at a given time, and three phases of Russian experience are shown in their work. For many readers Tolstoy is the most marvellous, because to enjoy his finest work is to undergo a rebirth of the senses. Tolstoy's perpetual theme is resurrection, as it was later to be Pasternak's, and as more agonizingly it is Dostoevsky's. The supreme quality in Russian writing one might call rejuvenescence. There is always a way back to innocence and spontaneity. This above any writer Tolstoy demonstrates, even in the last moments of Anna Karenina. As her head awaits the wheel, glimpses of childhood and girlhood restore fleetingly to life all the joys she had once known.

8

Saltykov-Shchedrin: *The Golovlyov Family*

THE only work by the greatest of Russian satirists after Gogol to be at all well known in English is a novel, *The Golovlyov Family* (1880). M. E. Saltykov (1826–1889), who took the pen-name Shchedrin, first began writing after the Crimean War when he returned from seven years' exile in Vyatka, where Herzen had been before him. Saltykov belonged to the Petrashevsky circle like Dostoevsky but was sent away before the catastrophe in 1849. He reached high rank in the Civil Service which he did not leave until after he had served on the editorial board of *The Contemporary*. He then worked with Nekrasov on *Fatherland Notes* which succeeded *The Contemporary* as the main organ of opposition. After Nekrasov's death in 1878 he carried on for six years alone until his journal was suppressed and Saltykov felt he had dropped out of literature. Not one of his fellow-writers, he complained, had a word of sympathy for him. 'That is why I remembered Turgenev who would not have acted in this way.' Saltykov had lived for literature and now he appeared to have 'lost his chance of conversing every month with the reader'. He was still to publish a few books including his celebrated Fables. But Saltykov's role as publicist and educator seemed to have largely gone.

This was the man of whom Turgenev said in 1881: 'Do you know, it sometimes seems to me that the whole of our literature rests on his shoulders.'[1] If it did, the foreign reader has been strangely ignorant of a most important figure in the succession. Turgenev had long admired

Saltykov. In 1871 he wrote for *The Academy* a note to inform the English public about one of Saltykov's most effective satires, *The History of a Town*. This was a mock chronicle, on the lines of Pushkin's *History of the Village of Goryukhino*, presenting a grotesque scene of misgovernment, brutality and chaos. Turgenev found 'something of Swift' in Saltykov: 'that serious and grim comedy, that realism—prosaic in its lucidity amidst the wildest play of fancy—and, above all, that constant good sense—I may even say that moderation—kept up in spite of so much violence and exaggeration of form'. Saltykov's lucidity was that of a consistent democrat who held before him a single purpose—to harry the government—and who knew his Russia, as Turgenev allowed, 'better than any man living'. This was a different knowledge from Leskov's: it embraced the official classes (whom he could attack from a position of strength as their former successful colleague, and with Gogol's weapons), the landed gentry and the village. Saltykov had an historical sense, a power of analysis, which made him a reliable witness for the economic and social historian in years to come. He conceived of literature as Belinsky had done, and like the men with whom he had worked on *The Contemporary*. 'Literature and propaganda', he said, 'are one and the same thing.' It was to lead public opinion through the darkness of the present towards a bright future. When Turgenev speaks of him as carrying the whole weight of literature it must be in the sense of keeping up a standard of truth and of responsibility towards the public.

For some thirty years Saltykov turned his intelligence upon those 'accursed questions' abounding in Russian life. He had an irrepressible comic gift, a remarkable talent for parody, an ear for the varieties of popular and official speech and the knack of inventing derisive names for what he disliked and finding phrases that travelled far. There was no more skilled publicist in Russian letters: even Dostoevsky, his lifelong opponent, must yield him place. This very success entails, of course, its own limitation: Dostoevsky's

Diary of a Writer was written, as it were, with his left hand. As a novelist Saltykov cannot compete with him, partly because he lacked Dostoevsky's poetic insight, his myth-building powers. However, *The Golovlyov Family* is a distinguished novel, and in it the publicist more than once transcends his own prose.

Saltykov's theme is the decay, both material and moral, of a landowning family. The Golovlyovs, as the Russian title states, have been 'masters', and the story opens not long before the abolition of serfdom. Their present wealth and power have come to them through the exertions of Arina Petrovna, the dominant mother of three sons, who has practically driven her husband to the impotence of a sickbed. At sixty she is 'still vigorous and accustomed to live exactly as she pleases'. All her thoughts have gone to building up the family fortunes, and yet the family for which she has 'deformed her entire life' is a mere abstraction to her, a nonentity. This theme of the emptiness that lies in wait to swallow up her activity is pursued to its tragic conclusion through the novel, which becomes more than the political satire its author may have intended. At the close we are to discover, with her broken grandchild Anninka, that the Golovlyov house is

> death itself, evil and empty-mawed: death perpetually awaiting a new victim.

And one by one the victims pass into the emptiness. First there is the eldest son, the incapable Styopka who has wasted his substance and returns to his mother's house to die a drink-crazy prisoner:

> In the morning he would wake with the light, and with him there woke anguish, revulsion, hatred. Hatred un-protesting and without reason, hatred for something indefinite and formless . . . Not one thought, not one desire. In front of his eyes the stove—and his thought became so overfilled with its presence there that he took in no other impressions. Then the window replaced the

stove, window, window, window . . . Nothing mattered,
nothing, nothing mattered . . . He must wait for night so
as to break through again to those blessed moments when
earth vanished from under his feet and instead of four
wearisome walls there opened before his eyes a limitless
shining void.

(I. 'The Family Tribunal')

The void awaits Arina Petrovna herself. In the second
chapter, ten years having passed, she has been dislodged
from power by the unscrupulous Porfiry, her second son.
Already

The family fortress, raised by the tireless hands of Arina
Petrovna, has crumbled,

though she does not notice it. The youngest son is now
dying of drink and misery. Thereafter, driven to take
refuge on the small estate of her two orphaned grand-
daughters, Arina Petrovna suddenly finds herself 'a ruin'
and she too faces the vacancy that had extinguished her
eldest son:

. . . She sat in an armchair before a table on which
were laid frowsty cards, and she dozed. Then she would
tremble, wake up, look out of the window, and for a
long while without any conscious thought she would not
take her eyes off the endlessly stretching distance.
Pogorelka was a gloomy estate . . . But since Arina
Petrovna had lived from childhood almost without a
break in the country, this poor landscape not only never
struck her as monotonous but it even spoke to her heart
and stirred the remains of feelings that were still warm in
her. The best part of her being lived in these bare and
endless fields, and her gaze instinctively sought them at
any time. She would stare at the immensity of fields,
stare at the sodden villages, which in the form of black
dots here and there chequered the landscape; would
stare at the white churches in village graveyards, would
stare at the speckled stains cast on the flat fields by clouds

wandering in the rays of the sun, would stare at that unknown peasant who walked down the furrows in a field, and it seemed to her that he had stuck in one place.

But all the time she thought of nothing. . . .
(III. 'Family Scores')

The family fate is summed up as 'idleness, unsuitability for any work whatsoever, and drink'. Arina Petrovna who married into the family escapes the last, but long before death she suffocates in the futile pettiness of her son's mind. He, Porfiry or Iudushka ('little Judas') as his brothers had called him, concentrates the greed and heartlessness of the Russian landowner at his worst—and this book was directed against the landowners as a class. Porfiry is likened to a spider who at the end spins his web round the poor in fantasy as once he had done in fact; he sits at the heart of a void which spreads out from him to envelop others. Porfiry might be called a more abandoned Karenin, who has put himself by the power of empty words outside all normal life. When Arina Petrovna dies

> he did not understand that the grave opened before his eyes was carrying away his last link with the living world, the last living person with whom he could share the dust that filled him. And henceforward this dust, finding no outlet, would gather in him until the time when eventually it would choke him.

(IV. 'The Niece')

Saltykov claims Porfiry to be 'not so much a hypocrite as a sneak, a liar and a windbag'. He cannot be called a hypocrite because he has no sense of any principles to feign: they don't in Russia produce 'champions and propagandists of various social principles, but they just leave us to grow as nettles grow by the fence'. Porfiry spends many hours praying in front of the ikons: 'he had studied to perfection the technique of standing at prayer'. This activity is soon revealed as another protective form of idleness. He has one concern only:

. . . Iudushka was prepared in advance *for everything*.
He knew that *nothing* would catch him unawares and
nothing would make him in any way retreat from the
mesh of empty and utterly putrid aphorisms in which he
had wrapped himself from head to foot. For him there
existed neither grief, nor joy, nor hatred, nor love.

(III. 'Family Scores')

Gradually as the Golovlyov house falls into his power he
gives way to the family vice, drunkenness—which for him
means at first a spiritual and moral drunkenness. Like
Gogol's Manilov he comes to inhabit a world of unbroken
fantasy, and when reality threatens him in the form of a
son whom he can save from dishonour and suicide by lending
him a little money, Porfiry tries to lay the spectre with
words. Meaningless aphorisms are his refuge that never
fails.

Porfiry, at first an unknown quantity for Arina Petrovna,
a disquieting form on the outskirts, moves rapidly to the
centre. Even in the second of Saltykov's seven chapters the
light falls mainly on him. The last phase of the Golovlyov
household brings his complete dominion: every detail of
the meaningless life that goes on there originated with
Porfiry. The scenes are symbolic: November night, the
blizzard outside obliterating village, church and forest; and
round the samovar, playing a children's card game and
talking comfortable platitudes, the old woman now submissive, the garrulous son and his dull mistress. Porfiry
soothes all three of them with baby-talk. This idle, self-
perpetuating rhetoric of Iudushka acquires a dreadful life
of its own—all through the latter half of the book his
incessant voice is to be heard, marvellously inventive in
nonsense. Saltykov was a great parodist: Porfiry's jargon,
propped up on diminutives that somehow suggest the waving
legs of a centipede, catches the essence of a particularly
Russian cant. There is no stopping this voice. As Anninka,
the last of the younger generation, realizes: 'You had to
submit. Triviality [*poshlost*] is immensely strong. . . .'

The novel makes an indictment, but in the best tradition of satire it sees the culprit as his own victim. This emerges most clearly from the consideration of Anninka, one of two orphan girls brought up by their grandmother at Pogorelka, the 'gloomy estate'. Anninka, born a lady and a proprietress, takes to the stage, does not succeed, follows her sister who has also failed on the stage into the misery of being a kept woman; the sister is cast off and commits suicide; Anninka returns to the Golovlyov house consumptive and a dipsomaniac. Before the final collapse of her hopes she comes back to stay with Iudushka and to visit Arina Petrovna's grave. Anninka's predicament is finely rendered throughout, but never more so than when after the memorial service she takes tea with the priest. In his parlour all is drabness, despondency, want; the priest, though still a young man, has grown gaunt and hopeless; his wife is sick from child-bearing.

None the less Anninka could not help noticing that even these broken, exhausted and poor people regarded her not as a normal parishioner, but rather with pity as a lost sheep.

There follows a scene in which the priest's wife, with genteel but remorseless curiosity about the way actresses live, torments the lost sheep. Saltykov gets exactly the feelings of each person in this excruciating comedy: Anninka at first patient and a little at a loss how to reply, but soon eager to escape; the priest gently reproachful, his wife insistent:

'There is one thing more I wanted to ask . . . we have a girl in the parish . . . she was maid to an actress in Petersburg. They live well, she said, actresses do, only every month they have to procure a ticket . . . is that so?'

(IV. 'The Niece')

The priest tries to smooth it over, but the mischief is out: the priest's wife, like the servants at Pogorelka, believes that Anninka has a prostitute's yellow ticket.

Saltykov's human insights are backed by a sure understanding of the social case. Anninka's difficulties owe not a little to the defects in her education, which he describes as a 'high school–light opera' business with the stress mainly on light opera. Although his general tone is so much more severe than George Eliot's, the comment recalls what she said about Rosamond Vincy and Miss Lemon's establishment. And indeed Saltykov shows a moral vigilance like George Eliot's when it comes to the crisis for Anninka. He compares the resolution needed to change one's course in life with that of a suicide—'only it is more difficult. Here you must destroy your previous life, yet after destroying it live on.' Anninka is incapable of the long discipline for recovery. Nor can she find support in her background. Pogorelka has no attractions, except the mushrooms in summer; at Golovlyovo emptiness and that empty vessel Iudushka lie in wait. Again like George Eliot, Saltykov admits an iron law of cause and effect. The philosophy of his novel—its grounding in social science—is set out almost in the last pages:

> There are families over whom hangs a kind of fatality. This is particularly to be seen among the petty gentry, who having no work, no bond with the common life and no political importance, at first sheltered under the defence of serfdom, strewn over the face of the Russian land, and now, defenceless, live out their time in crumbling manors. In the life of these wretched families both success and failure are something blind, unforeseen, unconsidered.
>
> (VII. 'The Reckoning')

Saltykov wants his novel to be understood as dealing with representative facts.

At the same time he was hostile towards *le naturalisme* which he censured for the same reasons as Henry James in his essay on Maupassant. Naturalism simplifies; it diminishes the scope of life to the merely animal; and—for Saltykov—it does not grasp the meaning of history. All Russian writers seem endowed with an exceptional sense of history.

The broad humane tradition in his native literature kept Saltykov from the wrong use of statistics. Nobody (unless it was Gleb Uspensky, the most talented of the populist writers) understood better the new patterns of village life, for example; his sketch of the *miroed* or village usurer has complete authority; yet, although much of his work— including *The Golovlyov Family*—begins with the sketch form, he is far more than a social historian. At its finest Saltykov's writing displays a moral depth in which indignation merges with tragic pity.

The final scene in which Porfiry and his niece during Holy Week contemplate the meaning of the Passion illustrates this. By now Porfiry, alone with Anninka in the darkness of Golovlyovo, has become a physical and moral wreck. He has learned from her the family vice—alcoholism. And then suddenly conscience, so long out of view, stirs and stings him. After the service he broods as never before on what he has heard—the message of forgiveness— and resolves to visit his mother's grave in penitence. Now at last he feels pity for Anninka:

> . . . he stroked her head.
> 'Poor one! my poor one!' he uttered in a low voice.
> At this contact something unexpected came over her. To begin with she was astonished, but gradually her face began to distort and distort, and suddenly a whole torrent of dreadful hysterical sobs surged up from her chest.
> 'Uncle? are you a good man? tell me, are you a good man?' she almost shouted.

Porfiry cannot possibly be construed as a good man, yet at least he tries to amend for all the wrong done by him— the death of his mother, the suicide of the two sons he cut off, the riddance of an illegitimate child—when that night he goes out on pilgrimage to Arina Petrovna's grave.

> Outside there was a wind and a wet March blizzard swirled around, sending into the eyes whole showers of

melting snow. But Porfiry Vladimirovich went down the road, stepping into puddles, and feeling neither snow nor wind, though instinct made him wrap tighter his dressing-gown.

The next day early in the morning, from the village near the cemetery where Arina Petrovna was buried, there galloped a messenger with the news that a few paces from the highroad had been found the frozen corpse of the master of Golovlyovo. They rushed to tell Anninka, but she lay on her bed in a state of unconsciousness, with all the symptoms of high fever. Then they equipped a new rider and sent him to [Porfiry's female cousin] who ever since last autumn had been watching keenly all that happened at Golovlyovo.

So ends one of the darkest novels in Russian literature. Its austerity and relentless logic seem to belong rather to the French imagination. This might have been written by the Mauriac of *Thérèse Desqueyroux*. Saltykov too at the end of his story invokes the Christian understanding. It alone can make out what is human in so much hardness of heart and depravity.

Saltykov wrote this novel over the course of five years (1875–80) amid much polemical journalism and effective satire. It is pre-eminent in his work for its passion and moral depth, though some aspects of his genius—notably an often outrageous fantasy—are to a large extent missing from it. In the satire that followed, *A Modern Idyll*, Saltykov develops on Swiftian lines the paradox that the subjects of Alexander III can prove their reliability in one way only—by crime (which is not an ideological activity). Being a satirist he likes to press hard some dominant notion: satire more than most literary forms radiates from an idea. The 1870's and 1880's in Russia abounded in ideas and arguments. Through most of his career Saltykov carried on a running dispute with Dostoevsky. His own position was simple: 'Given a marsh, there will be goblins.' To exorcize the evil spirits you must clear away the marsh, which for

him meant the existing order of society. A less hopeful
mind such as Dostoevsky's would accept the marsh as
irremovable. Saltykov's conviction makes for strength
and simplicity. He is not equal in stature to Dostoevsky,
nor ever claimed to be. Yet among writers of a more
limited kind—those who believe literature can serve
politics—Saltykov-Shchedrin holds a most honourable
place. He wrote for the coming democracy, for 'Ivanushka'
who, he knew well enough, could not read him, being
illiterate. Saltykov like Swift had the prose intelligence to
its highest capacity. He is distinguished by vigour, comic
invention and strong sense. In *The Golovlyov Family* he
adds a steadiness of moral vision which almost passes into
poetry. It finds memorable images, and the style is intent and
rapid.

9

Dostoevsky: the dialectic of resistance

WHAT sets Dostoevsky (1821–1881) apart from all other novelists of his day is a fearful experience: his arrest, condemnation to death, reprieve on the scaffold; then eight years of prison labour and military service in Siberia. The Petrashevsky circle (broken up on 23 April 1849) has been described by Professor Venturi as 'a strange, circumscribed society':

> Their attitude and conduct lack the width of Moscow [that is, of Herzen and Bakunin], and reflect rather the narrowness of the bureaucratic capital of Nicholas I's great empire. . . . Theirs was a mass of mistaken ambitions and readiness for sacrifice, of immense hopes and small means, of petty passions and great ideals.[1]

He concludes that Dostoevsky (already known for his humanitarian novel of 1846, *Poor Folk*, which had much moved Belinsky) was drawn to these Friday meetings of Fourierists and doctrinaire socialists because the year 1848 had 'interested him as drama'. In the Peter and Paul Fortress Dostoevsky said, one would think sincerely, at his examination:

> . . . this system [Fourier's] is harmful, first, simply by being a system; secondly, however exquisite, it remains the most unrealizable Utopia.

It is noteworthy that he should meet head-on one of the principal enthusiasms of his age and soon turn away from it; that he should approach the master ideas of the century by way of an ill-informed and passionate sect, deeply provincial, and unstable in their views; that, finally, he should work out, in solitude and against the prevailing trend, his own equally passionate and some would urge equally unbalanced counter-philosophy.

For that is the root fact about Dostoevsky: his opposition. After the ordeal he emerged as a sceptic where others believed, a believer (with agonies of misgiving) in the religion that many leading minds had now done with. Tolstoy opposed the age, too; but as it were from a distance, partly in the name of the old Muscovite order, partly as a great nobleman who could take his own path. For Dostoevsky the struggle was closer and internecine: he fought his adversary on the same terms, and superficially he has much in common with Pomyalovsky (1835–1863) or Saltykov-Shchedrin. Like them he writes mainly of the educated but poor and unprivileged, not often indeed like Saltykov of the peasants, but of the 'thinking proletariat' and petty officials. In his demotic style he resembles Pomyalovsky and Gleb Uspensky. In subject and method he belongs to the 'left wing' of literature; hence the peculiar pain of his relations with the radical camp for whom he was always the renegade. Dostoevsky, then, is the plebeian (*razno-chinets*) at odds with the philosophy of his fellows.

> The evil lurks deeper down in humanity than the socialist physicians reckon . . . in no order of society will you eliminate evil . . .[2]

Here he stands apart from Tolstoy no less than from the radicals. Evil for them was something to be put right by knowing the truth—a moral truth as to which, though differing about the means, they were agreed. But Dostoevsky saw evil and irrationality as inexpungible from the nature of man. And whereas most of his contemporaries judged 'nihilism' as a political idea—a good or a bad instrument for liberation—Dostoevsky held it to be a temptation to evil. His main attack on nihilism came with *The Devils* (1871), but ever since he wrote *Notes from the Underworld*

(1864) the nightmare of an order in which 'all things were permissible' had engaged his imagination. According to Rozanov[3] his first moral discovery (revealed in *Notes from the Underworld*) convinced him of irrationality as a right which no utopian system like Fourier's ever allowed for. The second discovery, made in *Crime and Punishment* (1866), affirms the inviolability of human life. Raskolnikov in murdering the old money-lender found that he had murdered himself. Armed with these two principles—the right of men to be capricious and even vile, since they are not perfectible, and the sanctity of the human person—he opposed the builders of socialism (the 'crystal palace'). They had overlooked the 'underground man' whose viciousness is a malady to be cured only by the Christian gospel. One question Dostoevsky must face over and over again—he faces it for the last time in his definitive work *The Brothers Karamazov*: does God exist? That is the choice: submission to the living God, or a moral chaos in which all things are permissible.

In *The Brothers Karamazov* (1881) the whole thought of Dostoevsky is to be found. Whereas Tolstoy's last major novel *Resurrection* shows a narrowing down of his genius, and Turgenev's last major novel *Virgin Soil* was written partly from hypothesis, *The Brothers Karamazov* includes and surpasses all Dostoevsky's previous work. Like *Crime and Punishment* it deals with murder and retribution; Alyosha is an innocent of the same kind as Prince Myshkin in *The Idiot*; Smerdyakov is an 'underground man', a degraded malignant; Ivan Karamazov has much in common with Stavrogin and Kirillov, the arrogant and tormented rationalists of *The Devils*; there are suffering children, scenes of frenzy and outrage, destructive passions between men and women, the same gnawing questions and metaphysical debates; and lastly in Ivan's 'Legend of the Grand Inquisitor' a myth is perfected that Dostoevsky had been carrying with him for many years. This was the novel which all his life he had been preparing to write, and as Gide says he had the rare good fortune of Rembrandt and

Beethoven who also 'went forward from work to work'. 'No withering in this fiery old age . . . a steady and violent aggravation of thought.'[4] More was intended: Dostoevsky planned the novel we have as prelude to a vaster construction which would show Alyosha the saint in action. He died only three months after finishing the first stage of an inconceivable book which aspired in its sequel to be practically the fifth gospel.

No Russian writer belonged more to his age than Dostoevsky, whose imagination was bred not only on Schiller and the 'Gothic' school but also on the daily newspapers, with their stark record of crime and misery. *The Brothers Karamazov* was above all a tract for the times, in which he would concentrate 'all the horror of our age'. 'No community, no culture, everything breaking down into its primal elements.' Once again he begins with fact—the true story of a convict he had known in Siberia wrongly sentenced for parricide when his own brother had been guilty. Given the situation—of antagonism between members of one family—Dostoevsky refashions it to invent a drama with the highest symbolic value. There are five Karamazovs, the father and four sons (one of them illegitimate). They share an attitude to life which both Ivan and the Public Prosecutor distinguish—a reckless animal energy, a nihilistic force: even Alyosha the youngest brother is not wholly exempt from this. At the same time they represent various faculties or potentialities of man: Ivan the intellect, Dmitry the passional self, Alyosha the spiritual, Fyodor Pavlovich the sensual nature, Smerdyakov bestiality. Thus the story achieves a kind of abstraction only to be compared with that other and more recognizable allegory, *Moby Dick*. Yet the abstraction which leads easily on to the crowning myth, Ivan's 'Legend cf the Grand Inquisitor', is used to organize a whole mass of richly apprehended circumstance. Dostoevsky's novel is able to combine a pellucid scheme with remarkable density of detail.

It has often been pointed out, for instance, that the most metaphysical part of the novel—Book V with Ivan's 'revolt' and his myth of the Grand Inquisitor—has for its setting a tavern, in which

> there went on all the customary tavern hubbub, shouts calling for service could be heard, the uncorking of beer bottles, the knock of billiard balls, the drone of an organ.

The Brothers Karamazov takes place in a shabby provincial town, as does *The Devils*. Such places are mean replicas of the great city (which for Dostoevsky is St Petersburg, the scene of *Crime and Punishment* and *The Idiot*). Even beyond Gogol and Nekrasov he is the master of urban detail; like Dickens, the poet of a fallen world, the nineteenth-century metropolis. To Jane Austen's heroine in *Mansfield Park*

> sunshine appeared . . . a totally different thing in a town and in the country. Here, its power was only a glare: a stifling sickly glare, serving but to bring forward stains and dirt that might otherwise have slept.

So Fanny sees

> the walls, marked by her father's head . . . the table cut and notched by her brothers, where stood the tea-board never thoroughly cleaned, the cups and saucers wiped in streaks, the milk a mixture of motes floating in thin blue, and the bread and butter growing every minute more greasy. . . .
>
> (xlvi)

Add to the painful particularity of her vision a more acutely felt homelessness; multiply Portsmouth a few times to get the prison bulk of St Petersburg; and you have the pitiless scene in which Marmeladov the broken clerk, Sonya the unwilling prostitute, Raskolnikov the student utterly alone, try to make sense out of their lives among the multitude of the 'humiliated and oppressed'. Dostoevsky seems to acknowledge no other world than the town great or petty. His images are of necessity urban: the devil who appears to Ivan Karamazov looks and behaves like a genteel sponger in brown jacket, check trousers and soiled cravat. Dostoevsky finds his material in the newspapers: for him the diurnal and fantastic spell out a 'realism in the highest sense'. He mediates the city, and uses the dialect of the city, making the common style adopted by the intelligentsia vibrate with his own passion.

Dostoevsky's style is (at the first glance) without distinction. Many critics, among them Belinsky and Dobrolyubov, with the support here of Tolstoy, have complained that his characters all speak in the same voice—Dostoevsky's own. Dobrolyubov analysed two pages of a girl's conversation from *The Humiliated and the Oppressed*, and found it monotonous, bookish and turgid: he concluded that Dostoevsky had too shallow a stock of observations, that the characters, though keenly scrutinized, were dreary and thin.[5] Yet—certainly if we are to speak of the greatest novels, *The Brothers Karamazov* in particular—these objections fall to the ground. Not only does the graceless, untidy, but insistent Russian of Dostoevsky hold you from the first moment, but every voice, when you listen attentively to his characters, has its own marked accent. Dostoevsky's instinct, as George Steiner reminds us, was wholly dramatic; and a contemporary has witnessed that he had no rival as reader:

> In a thin but piercingly distinct voice that held you beyond description he read one of the most marvellous chapters in *The Brothers Karamazov*—'The Confession of a Burning Heart'—Mitya Karamazov's story of how Katerina Ivanovna came to him for money to save her father. Never before had I observed such a dead silence in the hall, such a total absorption of the emotional life of a crowd a thousand strong in the moods of a single man.[6]

Dostoevsky's people are always inspired to astonishing thought and express themselves with an abandonment that shocks the Western reader. And though his work teems with abstraction—Berdyaev has called him the greatest of Russian philosophers—yet these metaphysical views are not to be divorced from the characters who utter them, and each arises out of a lived situation. Dostoevsky's novels show always 'the passion of the special case'.[7] In them great questions are dramatized: extraordinary questions through the experience of ordinary people amid squalor and mediocrity.

Dobrolyubov also complained that too many of Dostoevsky's characters are submissive and unwilling to assert their full rights as men. (Belinsky had been in raptures over the scene in which Devushkin, of *Poor Folk*, showed such immense gratitude to the general for recognizing that he too was a human being.)[8] Dostoevsky's world is more or less divided between two types of person: the cruel and the meek, the predators and their victims. Such a grand simplification (however deep the passion that lies behind it) has manifold dangers. In part this reading of life may have come to him through his experience of the convicts; or it may have been prompted by everything he saw in Russia, where tyranny and long-suffering have faced each other for centuries. Dostoevsky wishes to recommend the meek: the hero by design of *The Brothers Karamazov* is Alyosha, and to offset Ivan's rebellion Father Zosima (so Dostoevsky hoped) would convince the reader of a heavenly wisdom 'to the Greeks, foolishness'. But Ivan dominates, and necessarily, because Alyosha and his preceptor Zosima (though the latter was drawn from living models) lack nourishment from their time: whereas all its energy, pride, confidence, all its essential anarchy and ruthlessness, pour into Ivan: he embodies the age or (more accurately) one of its great temptations which worked powerfully upon Dostoevsky's mind—the temptation to be self-sufficient in a state where 'all things are permissible'. And Dostoevsky takes a risk with Ivan similar to Milton's with Satan: he allows him a dangerous prominence, since the episode of his rebellion concentrates the book's whole meaning; and trusts that Zosima's sweetness will then prevail, with an aftersense to cancel Ivan's blasphemy. But the rank vitality of Ivan, his love for 'the sticky buds of spring', move us more strongly than anything Zosima or Alyosha can plead. All that he is they seem to deny, and therewith to cut out that elemental self which engages us with the struggle to live.

There are two centres to the book—Ivan's protest against the order of this world and his myth of the Grand Inquisitor forming the metaphysical centre, and the murder which Ivan has willed, Smerdyakov committed, and Mitya finally accepted as his own deed, forming the centre or mainspring of its action. Rozanov insisted that the metaphysical centre has only the weakest link with the story, and can be judged on its own (though expressing 'the soul of the entire work'). Yet the protest and the myth are not to be separated from Ivan; only Ivan, in his situation and with his character, could have uttered them. And the doctrine he there expounds must be seen as issuing in the murder: Smerdyakov is the under-self or degraded disciple of Ivan, bearing to him much the relation of Verkhovensky in *The Devils* to Stavrogin. The action of the entire book, then, falls into the perspective of Ivan's thesis: his suffering and that of his brothers bring it to the test.

Dostoevksy constructed this novel, like its predecessors, with a skill that may not at once be apparent. The first book, entitled *The History of a Family*, announces one principal theme—the degeneration of family life. Fyodor Pavlovich, the father, is presented in his corruption as no freak but a national type. And his disunited family, bound together by the chance of a common progenitor and their Karamazov qualities, marks a new turn in Russian civiliza-tion—the rootless world of the nineteenth century. The only hope for this family, as in a fairy-tale, is to come from the third son Alyosha. The first two books serve to reveal him in sharp relief against his father and brothers.

Alyosha and Smerdyakov represent the two extreme poles in human nature—and Ivan, the intellect and imagina-tion of this family, is drawn towards both. Hence the importance of Book 5, 'Pro and Contra'—the title bears witness to the ceaseless dialectic that runs like a wild energy through the novel. In Book 5 Ivan confronts as it were the philosophies that result in Alyosha and Smerdyakov, submission and the blind will, order and anarchy. After his myth has been told Ivan heads towards anarchy and the blind will. And although Smerdyakov actually commits the crime, he does this with the sanction of Ivan. This kind of dialectical relation between his characters appealed very much to Dostoevsky. For him a man and his opposite are complementary and indeed closely united—as later Ivan will be with the devil whom he has himself conjured up from his imagination, yet who exists with all the reality appropriate to one half of a split mind.

In the same way one phase of the action is pitted against another. Book 6, 'A Russian Monk', answers—or seeks to answer—the perplexities of Ivan, when we encounter the *starets* Zosima carrying on 'a quiet and serene conversation' with his visitors. The method is orchestral—the playing of theme against theme, drawing out ideas through their opposition. Here then follows the restoring process of faith —in its turn to be rudely shaken by the physical decomposition of the holy Zosima's corpse, from which a miracle had been expected. The narrative leads us to no certainty— each position contains hidden within it the negation: we must accept the full deployment or nothing. And so Book 6 opening in peace returns to the panic and bewilderment with which Alyosha had broken in on the conversation. Alyosha, unsettled by the discovery, has to confront Rakitin the sceptic, who intrudes upon him like the hallucinatory devil upon Ivan. Alyosha ironically in reply uses Ivan's very words—'I do not rebel against my God, simply *I do not accept his world.*'

So Dostoevsky constructs his drama through the stages of a lived or suffered argument. The novel is a prolonged debate, and the issues it raises, though primarily religious, bear on the political destinies also of Russia and of human society in Dostoevsky's age. Whereas other novelists Saltykov-Shchedrin, for instance) wage one side of the argument, Dostoevsky centres the whole debate in his own mind, *Pro* and *Contra*, and encloses it in a single work. On the one side, those like Rakitin and Ivan whose own egoism destroys him; on the other, those like Zosima or Alyosha who have found 'the truth'; and between them, Mitya and Grushenka, impulsive, living in the moment, sensual and generous, who are drawn inexorably to the truth of feeling, just as that other sensualist, Fyodor Pavlovich, who respects no human being apart from himself, is dragged down by his egoism to perdition at the hands of Smerdyakov, the son most resembling him. Dostoevsky makes the struggle inside the Karamazov family a grand representative drama in which good and evil, faith and scepticism, love and rebellion, engage as principles, now manifest and now perplexed and fluid, in a supreme conflict. Once again the only possible comparison is with *Moby Dick*, but here the meaning never shows through nakedly, it is always grounded in and formed by the excesses of Russian life.

For in *The Brothers Karamazov*, even more than in his previous novels, Dostoevsky realizes that tendency of the Russian genius to seek truth through excess, and by extremes of self-assertion and self-abnegation. It had already been noticeable in the work of earlier novelists. Pechorin is an extremist; so is Oblomov; so are Bazarov and Iudushka Golovlyov. None of his predecessors could so control the opposing forces as Dostoevsky, unless it was Pushkin in *The Bronze Horseman*. This Dostoevsky does by the speed and energy of his onset. *The Brothers Karamazov* has not so much a structural design (though this is not lacking) as an unfailing equilibrium, which brings order perpetually into chaos, or saves chaos from itself. Dostoevsky's design is all a matter of adjustment, of compensation for one extreme by advancing its opposite. There is no core of steady living, no protected human norm, at the centre: rather a capacity on the part of the author himself to keep the most terrible passion sane, and thus cancel out the huge proportions of suffering and ecstasy so that the resultant sum is more or less in line with our expectations. By risking so much Dostoevsky preserves the essential human truth. In this way he comes at a balance through strain. It is a process peculiarly Russian.

Both Tolstoy and Dostoevsky achieve a completeness in the novel unsurpassed by the novelists of any literature. A completeness that involves not only breadth, which you find in Balzac, but also depth. It is a matter of the thoroughness with which they face experience; but Dostoevsky and Tolstoy, for all their common virtues, write a different novel. They share that immersion in their time which belongs, though the degree of it will vary, to all the main Russian novelists; *Anna Karenina* and *The Brothers Karamazov* both, as it were, wade through the 'seventies, catching up into their progress many issues and ideas that were then pressing and would now otherwise be forgotten. Both writers are at times publicists, seeking to drive controversy through the novel; both seek to interpret the destiny of Russia, and to that extent use the novel for prophecy. But their imaginative and intellectual powers work from opposite ends. Tolstoy sets at the centre of his work the norm: Levin to counteract Anna; Moscow to shame St Petersburg. Dostoevsky begins with the fantastic or the abnormal: an old woman murdered, or a father whom three of his sons wish to destroy. Then by entering into the case with an awareness of the normal human passions that are still to be found beneath the extraordinary facts, he proves through sharing the ordeal that such happenings lie at the very centre of man's experience. Truth is to be seized through ecstasy. And whereas Tolstoy conceives of an infallible touchstone, a state of mental and spiritual health, by which every excess can be corrected, Dostoevsky demands that life should be passionate and unstable, because only the dead can know stability. To live in the manner of Dostoevsky (as Blok did after him) all restraint must submit to feeling, which alone can bring truth. Gide was right in seeing a resemblance between Dostoevsky's thought and that of Blake in *The Marriage of Heaven and Hell*. For both the road of excess leads to the palace of wisdom.

Berdyaev has said that the coming of Dostoevsky changed Russian literature once and for all.[9] After his intervention what may be called the Pushkinian mode—the school of sanity, of confident humanism—has to battle for its life against the insurrection of Dostoevsky's 'underground man'. There is no such creature as Smerdyakov anywhere in Pushkin's vision; no such awakening to chaos and expectation of doom as constantly torments the people in Dostoevsky's books. Lawrence called him a marvellous seer but an evil thinker.[10] The evil shows more in his publicist writings, when he denounces Jews, Poles and Roman Catholics; when he maligns adversaries who cannot defend themselves, such as Chernyshevsky or Saltykov-Shchedrin; and writes to Pobedonostsev, whose lean fingers were almost to strangle free thought in Russia, about making 'our ideas' prevail. But, like Tolstoy, he was unable to resist the truth when once he had mobilized his imagination; then he demolishes all that had been tendentious—demolishes it in the last resort—and the novel burns away all that belonged to the politician, the nationalist and the false prophet. Dostoevsky cannot lie in the deepest parts of his novels: the realism he observes inevitably saves him from his own stratagems. Thus, to his own discomfort, the truth makes him free.

PART THREE

THE REVOLUTIONARY CRISIS

The beginning of modern times

BY 1880 in Western Europe, as in Russia, it had become clear that the heroic age of the novel was at an end. Flaubert and George Eliot both died in that year, Dostoevsky in 1881, Turgenev in 1883. A decade had already passed since the death of Dickens; nearly two must follow before Tolstoy would again publish a full-length novel. There are grounds for maintaining that our own epoch, or the one we lived in until recently, had its beginning at that time. The confidence of nineteenth-century positivism now started to waver; the childhood of industrial man had drawn to a close; new dangers and new difficulties multiplied. In Russia before the rest of Europe felt it disaster was in the air. Violence had been spreading throughout the 'seventies, and on 1 March 1881, an ominous date in Russian history, the terrorists finally struck down Alexander II. That explosion on the Catherine Canal, as Blok afterwards wrote,

> covered Russia with a cloud,

not to be dispersed until the Revolution of 1905. The years between were those recorded by Chekhov in all their apathy and frustration.

Dostoevsky, always sensitive to the hints of catastrophe, had written in 1878 to a group of students that Russia was 'trembling above the abyss'. His own novels showed amply the strain and hysteria threatening Russian life. One immediate result was that literature became fragmented. The short story seemed more appropriate to an age of petty concerns when the individual tended to live *incommunicado*. This, of course, would be the recurrent theme in Chekhov's work, that people cannot escape from their isolation.

The peculiar agitated sense of the 1880's is nowhere better expressed than in the short stories of Vsevolod Garshin (1855–1888).[1] The English reader has probably met his brilliant sketch *Four Days* about a wounded soldier in no-man's-land, which S. S. Koteliansky translated. Garshin, morbidly sensitive and plagued by the Russian intellectual's feeling of guilt before the people, had joined up for the campaign of 1876 against Turkey although hating war:

> The people go to war, we are obliged to go with them
> . . . War is immoral and horrible. We are obliged to take
> part in its immorality and horror.

The writer in arms made a very disturbing confession. It comes in a story entitled *From the Memoirs of the Ranker Ivanov* (1883). The troops on their way to the front are parading before Alexander II:

> . . . I don't remember the streets we went through, I
> don't remember if there were people in those streets and
> whether they watched us; I remember only the agitation
> that seized the soul, together with the consciousness of a
> terrible power in the mass to which you belonged and
> which drew you onward. One felt that for this mass
> nothing was impossible, that the current together with
> which I pressed forward and a part of which I formed
> could not know any obstacles, that it would break every-
> thing, overturn everything, destroy everything. And each
> one thought that the man before whom this torrent
> swept by could with a single word, a single gesture of his
> hand, change its direction, turn it back or again hurl it
> upon dreadful barriers; and each one wanted to find in
> the word of this sole man and the movement of his hand
> that unknown thing that led us to death. 'You could

lead us,' thought each one, 'to you we surrender our life;
look on us and be at peace; we are ready to die.'

And he knew that we were ready to die. He saw the
terrible, firmly advancing ranks of men, as they passed
by him almost at the double, men of his own poor
country, poorly clad, coarse soldiers. He sensed that they
all went to their death, calm and freed from responsibility. . . .

The writer Korolenko, who admired this passage for its
Tolstoyan power, commented on it:

> He [Garshin] had 'renounced his own ego', like the
> hero of his short story *The Coward*; had suppressed in
> himself both his rejection of war and many other
> rejections, had surrendered all this for some minutes of
> merging in the time-honoured sentiments of his people,
> for a rest from the grave responsibility that weighed on
> his whole generation. . . .[2]

Garshin, he saw, in thus yielding to an irresistible emotion,
an 'inhuman, fierce rapture', sought relief from his own
anxieties, standing as he did 'between two hostile worlds',
those of the government and the peasant masses. And the
whole experience was transitory: the sight of the Tsar
weeping with compassion for his troops

> came and went as though lit up momentarily by light-
> ning.

I have dwelt on this passage because already in 1883 it
foreshadows the dilemma of Russian writers in the Revolution. There were many inducements to give up the
responsibility of the artist and to regard his necessary
isolation as a weakness and even a crime. 'The revolution',
wrote Blok in March 1918, 'is not I alone, but we.' Or as
Hyacinth Robinson understood in *The Princess Casa-
massima*:

> there was joy and exultation in the thought of surrendering
> one's self to the wash of the wave, of being carried

higher on the sun-touched crests of wild billows than one
could ever be by a dry, lonely effort of one's own.[3]

With the twentieth century that 'dry, lonely effort' became
steadily more difficult. Our time has put unbearable
stresses on literature in all countries, but nowhere to the
extent of those borne by the Russian writer. Revolution,
reaction, world war; revolution, civil war, reaction, and
again world war—these overwhelming public events made
their terrible inroads into all private life; merely to keep
body and soul together in the first dark years used up all a
writer's energies; and then he found himself often faced
with the barren choice between conformity and exile. The
revolutionary crisis and its aftermath have now lasted for
half a century, and for twenty or thirty years before that it
was preparing. All this period prolongs the note of suffering
and exposure to ultimate trial which has become familiar
through Dostoevsky. It is truly the post-Dostoevskian
period of Russian literature.

Chekhov the humanist

OUR own critics at one time admired Chekhov to an absurd degree. 'Gentlemen', declared Middleton Murry,

> were I to confess the whole extent of my admiration of Anton Tchehov, I should be ashamed. It is an adoration. I know that he is not a great writer in the sense in which Tolstoy and Dostoevsky were. And yet I think he achieved a greater victory than they did.[1]

For Chekhov had gone out on

> the last of all forlorn quests: and he brings back the Grail in his hands.

Charles Du Bos compared him with Marcus Aurelius. 'Chekhov's English admirers', D. S. Mirsky complained, 'think that everything is perfect in Chekhov. To find spots in him will seem blasphemy to them.' There is an extra-ordinary appeal in Chekhov's image—the shy, almost virginal doctor with the pince-nez and hesitant cough—which captivated Tolstoy and which so many memoirs have confirmed that it is difficult to see the work apart from the engaging man. And because Murry, Katherine Mansfield and others surrounded Chekhov with a mystique, Lawrence was provoked to extravagance of the opposite kind:

> Tell your man Tchekhov is a second-rate writer and a willy wet-leg.[2]

One begins then with the legend of Chekhov: self-effacing, courteous, infinitely wistful. But the most cursory reading of his life or his correspondence will show that

Chekhov had also 'flint and iron' in him. The painter Repin on meeting him as a young man was reminded of Bazarov, 'positive, sane and healthy'. To get his intellectual character plain we should go back to the early 'sixties when Chekhov was still an infant. At that time the young novelist N. G. Pomyalovsky presented a new kind of hero in his novels *Plebeian Happiness* and *Molotov*. (The second of these impressed Turgenev, then working on *Fathers and Children*, and perhaps borrowing from it a hint or two for Bazarov.) The locksmith's son, Molotov, early orphaned and then taken charge of by a kindly professor, grows up to be self-reliant, honourable, clear-thinking. A member of Pisarev's 'intellectual proletariat', he practises the virtues by which the generation Chernyshevsky had educated was to live. By sheer hard work to gain independence; to respect yourself in the confidence of integrity; to trust in science; to face facts and despise rhetoric: these principles formed such people as Lenin's parents of whom Edmund Wilson wrote that 'this remarkable family, with their orderly and disciplined life, their habits of self-denial and their passion for education' seemed very like 'New Englanders of the plain-living and high-thinking period'.[3] It was such discipline, painfully acquired in a bleak boyhood, that gave the backbone to Chekhov—his unexpected severity.

Chekhov is like the fictional Molotov a plebeian: the serf's grandson who made a man of himself. As he wrote once in a famous letter:

> What writers of the aristocracy got free from nature, the plebeians buy with their youth.

> (January 1889)

The plebeian had to 'squeeze the serf out of himself drop by drop' until he could feel 'real human blood' in his veins. This long effort of self-improvement did not leave Chekhov dogmatic or harsh. He achieved instead a very unusual detachment and lucidity. Chekhov became a humanist in the tradition of Pushkin and Turgenev, like them valuing restraint, measure in all things; more concerned with perspective than hoping for any miracle of reformation. Understandably he did not care for Dostoevsky ('people aren't like that'): his allegiance went to the Tolstoy of before the crisis. And his mind was entirely secular: he shrugged off religion; and he would not even allow himself a compensating fervour in politics. Democrat by principle, he yet shows a reserve and fastidiousness that might fairly be termed aristocratic. It was no accident that Bunin, the last writer of the Russian gentry, should have become so intimate with Chekhov. At the same time he lacks the flippancy that a born aristocrat like Pushkin will sometimes adopt—*sprezzatura*, the nobleman's light disdain. Under his comedy, which comes near to farce, you can generally find an earnestness that recalls George Eliot and other middle-class Victorians.

He believed in the methods of medicine. Chekhov had taken a kind of Hippocratic oath to treat any subject with the rigour of a good diagnostician. So his fine impersonality comes from the dedicated doctor, a character that Chekhov sustained all though his writing life. Medicine we might say bred in him the classical temper, with its care for essentials, its lucidity and balance. Thus what Pushkin carried over from Voltaire and eighteenth-century sense and optimism, Chekhov found for himself in nineteenth-century science and also in the example of Pushkin and a few others. He became a highly disciplined writer, at a time when Russian literature had started to lose this virtue.

Chekhov began writing the humorous sketch for a public that never looked beyond journalism. With remarkable skill and imagination he transformed this trivial mode and won it a place in literature. Gogol's story *The Chaise* delighted him, and his earlier work aims at burlesque and nonsense. It was the veteran writer Grigorovich who first made him reckon seriously with his talent. As Chekhov grew more poignant and more profound, he still clung to the minor form. There are no full-length novels by Chekhov: his longest prose fictions reach the dimensions of a *povest'* or tale; the majority never exceed eight or ten pages.

(Garshin had met the same difficulty.) Chekhov as a story-teller never escaped altogether from the sketch. His more elaborate pieces, such as *The Steppe* (1888), rely on some device for connecting the sketches: there it was the journey and a small boy's awareness. And in theme too this would appear to be minor art. Chekhov the urban reporter touches briefly on the life of a young man who serves in a draper's shop, a chemist's wife or a chorus girl: the petty affairs of insignificant people, comic or pathetic. A waiter's health has collapsed, or an old coachman has lost his son, or an exhausted little maid smothers the baby she has been set to watch. Gogol and Dostoevsky had noted such incidents, but they were also capable of building on a grand scale. The age of Chekhov—those two decades passed over by history—substituted for the large view 'a broken bundle of mirrors'. It encouraged democratic art which meant naturalism. And this tended to cut down the possibilities of experience, seeking a small outlay with small returns. Chekhov might well have succumbed to the time. Yet he is not to be confused with the naturalist writers.

Sometimes indeed he talked in their style about the writer's duty to be indifferent. But this high clinical objecti-vity did not really suppress his feelings. It may have caused him to keep the instruments with which he worked bright and sharp: Chekhov's style favoured excision. He set him-self the aim not to accuse nor to indicate a way out—merely to put the case as simply and clearly as possible. Statement not prophecy—thus Chekhov focussed on immediate things, the ascertaining of fact. In 1890 he made an expedition to the penal settlement at Sakhalin and wrote a model report on his findings. This enterprise gives the clue to his other work. Chekhov wanted definition first: to pose the question without feeling obliged to solve it. And for presenting the case in its simplest terms—the evidence of the way in which people actually live—the short story was all he needed.

Big Volodya and Little Volodya (1893) shows the economy of his statement. In this story the scene that determines a young woman's life has taken place almost before she is aware of it. The newly mismarried wife believes in her happiness. She visits a nun who had once belonged to her own empty circle; suddenly she realizes that this presumed happiness is hollow; she throws herself at 'Little Volodya', her husband's friend with whom she had earlier been in love.

> After a week little Volodya abandoned her. And then life went on as before, just as uninteresting, unsatisfied and at times even tormenting. The colonel [her husband] and little Volodya played on and on at billiards and piquet, Rita told tasteless anecdotes badly, Sophia Lvovna [the wife] still used cabs and begged her husband to give her a troika ride.

All that will ever be significant has gone by. The case has been stated; there is no more to say, and judgement can now follow. Chekhov gives merely a brief unmitigated note of the outcome:

> Driving nearly every day to the convent she wearied Olya with complaints about her intolerable sufferings. She cried and all the time felt that she brought into the cell with her something unclean, pitiful and stale. And Olya told her in the mechanical tones of a lesson learned by rote that all this was nothing, all would pass and God would forgive.

Meanwhile life—Chekhov's feelings hardly come into this— does not forgive her. Waste cannot be made good. And waste—whether of talent or emotion or opportunity— pained and enraged Chekhov. A story like *The Grasshopper* (1892) about a wife who has never noticed the distinction of her doctor husband amid the bohemian riffraff she prefers to him is an indictment of waste. The rage there, as in other stories that have this obsessive theme, brings no outburst. Chekhov trained himself to a final reticence.

The Grasshopper was originally called *Philistines*. It made the contrast between two ways of living: that of the doctor, professional and altruistic—he 'served science and died from science'—and that of his wife and her set, frivolous and self-engrossed. These two ways confronted the plebeian intellectual like Chekhov himself: either to follow a hard calling in the face of every initial handicap, or to surrender, as did Ionych in the story of that name, who smothers his ideals and ends as a callous philistine. Perhaps no Russian writer felt more keenly than Chekhov the dreariness of a life without self-respect. In *Ward No. 6* the doctor who has compromised his beliefs is brought face to face with this betrayal by the madman whose confinement he eventually shares. The doctor has escaped from the philistine world around him, through a martyrdom that comes too late. *Ward No. 6* has a nightmare quality (which Lenin felt on reading it as a young man). The supreme horror for Chekhov is the nullity of a life misspent.

His pessimism recalls that of Garshin, both reflecting a dark time. The failure to communicate—so prominent in his plays—and the fact of solitude are virtually a law in his stories too. The bereaved cabman who can find no one to sympathize in the loss of a son; the bishop whose mother is too abashed to speak freely with him; the artist prevented from ever seeing again a young girl with whom he has fallen in love; the little boy writing to his grandfather in the country a letter that has no chance of reaching him: all suffer the same loneliness and frustration. When people do break through the barriers, as in *The Lady with a Little Dog* (1899), new obstacles await them:

> they both saw clearly that the end was a very long way off, and that the most complicated and difficult part was only just beginning.

Or if they are carried away by wild millennial dreams very soon the illusion has faded. So Laptev (in *Three Years*, 1895) tells his wife:

> 'In any case one must say goodbye to the idea of happiness ... I haven't got it. I never did have it and I'm sure

there is no such thing. However, once in my life I was happy when I sat at night under your umbrella. Do you remember how you forgot your umbrella once at my sister Nina's house? . . . At that time I was in love with you and I remember sitting the whole night long under this umbrella and feeling in a state of blessedness.'

The one moment of illusion, however absurd, retains its beauty. And what signifies in life—if it does signify—is always the incidental:

> The village of Ukleevo lay in a ravine, so that from the highroad and the railway station you could see simply the belfries and the chimneys of the linen factories. When passers-by asked what village this was they were told:
> 'This is the one where the deacon ate up all the caviare at a funeral.'
> . . . Many years had passed since that time, the deacon had long been dead, but they still remembered about the caviare. Whether life was so poor here, or people could notice nothing but this unimportant event which took place ten years before, they never had anything else to say about the village of Ukleevo.

> *(In the Ravine,* 1900)

But for the legend of this deacon you might expect the belfries and factory chimneys to sink for ever into the ground. Thus—in the manner of Gogol—a single grotesque incident, the four pounds of caviare consumed at a funeral feast, brings out all the dreariness of life; and Laptev's reference in the other story to the umbrella shows what an arbitrary and almost meaningless thing is human happiness. He denies that it exists at all; but, as we know from Chekhov's work in general, it makes here and there a fleeting, poignant appearance:

> At Oreanda they sat on a bench not far from the church, looked at the sea below and were silent. Yalta was scarcely visible through the morning haze, on the mountain-tops white clouds stood motionless. The foliage

did not stir on the trees, the cicadas were calling, and the monotonous hollow sound of the sea coming from below spoke of the rest, the everlasting sleep that awaits us. So it had sounded below when neither Yalta was here nor Oreanda, it sounds at present and will sound just like this, indifferent and hollow, when we are no more. And in this constancy, in its total indifference to the life and death of each one of us, is hidden perhaps the pledge of our eternal salvation, the uninterrupted movement of life upon earth, uninterrupted perfection. Sitting beside the young woman who looked so beautiful in the dawn, tranquillized as he was and enchanted by this fabulous setting—the sea, mountains, clouds, the broad sky— Gurov thought how really if you consider it everything is beautiful in this world, everything except what we ourselves think and do when we forget the highest aims of our being, and our own human dignity.

(*The Lady with a Little Dog*)

The stories have one clear advantage over the plays: their single focus which makes for a taut economy. The plays are filled with ruminant voices, or voices trying to break out of their solitude and remaining unheeded. In the stories his meaning can hardly be mistaken, as it so often has been in *The Cherry Orchard*. Chekhov's vision of life is no different, only the author himself can point things more surely, without having to depend upon the vagaries of actor and producer. The same delicate touches which illumine the plays are less likely to be lost in the stories. For instance, Gurov's lack of sympathy for the woman he has just seduced is brought out by one detail:

On the table in the hotel room was a melon. Gurov cut himself a piece *and unhurriedly began eating it*.

The revealing last phrase was added only in revision.[4] So too the banality of Anna Sergeevna's life at home is indicated by the grey fence opposite her house. It can be seen from earlier drafts of the stories that Chekhov had often been tempted to intrude. He was at heart a moralist and no less didactic than Saltykov-Shchedrin or even perhaps Chernyshevsky in *What Is To Be Done?* But as he had squeezed out of his veins the last drop of servile blood, so from his writing he expelled the sentimentalist. A piece of melon eaten unhurriedly takes the place of overt comment. Chekhov was able, as one writer put it, to convey 'through " a bottleneck glittering on the dam" the whole picture of a moonlit night'.[5] It is the same with moral statements. He had discovered the discipline of form, that 'true eloquence' (in Pascal's words) 'which mocks at eloquence'.

Chekhov's disengagement (not to be taken for the indifference of a naturalist) marks him off from his contemporaries and nearly all his successors. He felt involved in the national life and yet forced himself to avoid partisan zeal, pathos or the appeal to simplification. (*Doctor Zhivago* is a sustained tribute to Chekhovian practice.) He always set his emphasis on the personal—in nine cases out of ten, the petty. All around him generalization was in full swing. Even a humane and sensitive writer of the 'eighties like Gleb Uspensky tends always to see the individual case, which moves and shocks him, as representative. He is out finally to convince the reader by argument. Chekhov has no doctrine, only an attitude: his humanity, which he shares with Pushkin. Whatever incident he may describe matters very much to the people involved, and they matter to Chekhov, even though their history proves nothing but human weakness. He does not ignore social conditions and he may hint at political wrong; he knows well enough what it meant to work as a shop assistant or clerk for an old-fashioned despotic Moscow merchant (*Three Years*); and Corporal Prishibeev (in the story so named) stands as a brutal fact at the centre of a regime that may have seemed easy-going—for some. Chekhov would never accept the impersonal forces as an excuse: if people suffer, it is mainly their own fault. 'One can't go on living like this'; and indeed most of Chekhov's characters have the means to amend. They are not so poor or helpless that they need forfeit their human dignity. But mostly they do. People spend themselves to no purpose. Waste, waste—recriminations, tears and more waste. Like Laevsky in *The Duel* (1891) they come very slowly to recognize others as persons, and to understand that human beings are not expendable.

Purity is perhaps the word to describe Chekhov's aim, purity of outline and effect. The writing becomes pellucid, and even those stories that detail the emotional disorder of a spoilt life are not in themselves distraught: they breathe composure. Middleton Murry's claim for Chekhov as the master of a secret wisdom is sentimental. Chekhov achieved no victory beyond Tolstoy or Dostoevsky or for that matter Pushkin. Scale alone would settle his place in Russian literature: Chekhov has not their breadth and constructional power. Generally he falls short of mythical creation, though the three sisters who never get to Moscow and the family who lose their cherry orchard gain an obvious symbolic meaning. This can hardly be said of many characters in the stories. The latter note down with extreme purity and precision the moments in which something happened to an individual more or less obscure. Yet poetry is what many critics—Pasternak included—find pre-eminently in Chekhov. How are we to define that poetry? It comes down to proportion, to grace of feeling. Chekhov never loses sight of the vast background to human incident: the sea watched by two lovers on a bench, the storm impervious to the hatreds of men, the steppe in its loneliness. Thus he can achieve distance and relate: his impersonality rests on an awareness of physical space, and of the silence behind the discord. This gives him an impeccable touch, and his own kind of greatness.

11

Gorky and proletarian writing

'ASK any Russian intellectual today which modern writers attract the most public attention. The answer will be Anton Chekhov and Maxim Gorky.' The critic[1] who thus began his essay on Gorky in 1903 had to reckon with a prodigy and a portent. Even at the outset Gorky (1868–1936) belonged to legend—the man from the 'lower depths' who had found human worth and true freedom among tramps and outcasts (*bosyaki*). To separate the character from the legend is not easy. During the years Gorky played many parts—all of them, needless to say, sincerely. He was the first renowned proletarian writer; the 'stormy petrel', harbinger of revolution; the organizer of the new Soviet culture between 1918 and 1921; before and after this, the eminent man of letters living abroad; finally the Dean of Soviet Literature, who helped propagate the official doctrine, 'socialist realism'. He had known Tolstoy and Chekhov, Lenin and Stalin. At one time in the chaos following the Revolution and heightened by civil war he seemed to bear on his shoulders the entire weight of literary survival. Gorky stood for continuity. He helped to preserve both tradition and the lives of individual writers. Soviet literature had need of Gorky, even though some of its disabilities may have arisen through him.

The self-taught writer from the working class, exulting in his powers and eager for experience, is not likely to limit himself. Gorky began as a high romantic with the prose poem and fable (*The Song of the Falcon*, 1895; *The Old Woman Izergil*, 1895) and he continues so in a narrative like the famous *Birth of a Man* (1915):

133

The new inhabitant of the Russian land, a man of unknown destiny, lay in my arms and snored imperturbably. The sea splashed and murmured, all in white lacy shavings; the bushes whispered, the sun shone passing beyond noon.

We walked gently, and sometimes the mother halted sighing deeply and threw back her head, glanced away to sea, forest and mountains and then looked into her son's face: her eyes washed clean with the tears of suffering were once more amazingly clear, again they blossomed and burned with a deep blue flame of inexhaustible love.

Once halting she said:

'Lord God in heaven! How fine it all is! I'd like to walk this way on and on to the very end of the world, and he, my little son, would grow and grow in freedom, at his mother's breast, my own darling . . .'

. . . The sea goes on sounding . . .

This prose is deliberately rhythmic, near to the cadences of popular speech and the folk-tale; it encroaches on poetry. Much later in the essay *How I Learned to Write* (1928 Gorky admitted that his early work was often too ornate. Tolstoy and Chekhov pointed out to him the inaccuracies that went with this manner. Chekhov, so watchful of excess in his own writing, while he acknowledged Gorky's plastic power—'when you depict a thing, you see it and feel it with your hands'—told him he lacked restraint:

> You are like the spectator at the theatre who expresses his enthusiasm so unrestrainedly that he stops himself and others from listening.

> (December 1898)

Gorky could not altogether give up his lavishness and his love of gesture. 'A time has come', he explained to Chekhov in January 1900, 'that needs the heroic': people wanted 'stirring and vivid' pictures that would be 'loftier, better, more beautiful' than reality:

It is absolutely essential that present-day literature

should begin a little to heighten life, and as soon as it does life will heighten itself, i.e. people will live more quickly, vividly. But at present just look what vile eyes they have—dull, muddy, frozen.

This had been the point of his fable *The Siskin and the Woodpecker* (1893): the 'elevating lie' is preferable to the 'degrading truth'. Gorky's huge success at the start was due to his buoyancy, his enthusiasm for life, his unashamed rhetoric. Eventually he would abjure rhythmic prose—a mode rather less suspect in Russia where it had some grounding in popular speech—and cut out gratuitous images. But the classical temper, in spite of an admiration for Pushkin and Chekhov, could never be his. He inherited the gusto and the faults of Leskov. Against what Lawrence called 'purplism' he had a long struggle to wage, and undoubtedly Chekhov brought him to realize this. 'Everyone in the presence of Anton Pavlovich couldn't help wanting to be simpler and more truthful. . . .' So he confesses in the *Memoir*. Still, the 'picturesque' leanings persisted: he had the example of oral poetry from his own grandmother and he loved the embroidered shirt.

Yet there was a legitimate appeal in his writing about tramps and casual labourers face to face with the elements. 'The sea laughed': this phrase opening the story *Malva* (1897) has been much criticized, but for Gorky as for the folk-poets of the *byliny*, all nature joins in man's happiness or grief. Gorky is less the impressionist writer (like Chekhov or Bunin) than the expressionist. His imagination riots with images, not always well chosen; he welters in physical life; vividness and pungency are the effects he aims at. Gorky believed in man with the secure optimism of Browning, despite the degradation, brutality and squalor which he had known. He trusted in the social hope: if men would struggle enough they could live like the ballad heroes, miracle-workers who win all. His was an imagination that tended towards epic for the glorifying of human achievement. He rejected Dostoevsky: the evil for him lay in our history not in ourselves. No less feelingly than the populists Gorky believed that the unawakened masses had every potentiality of goodness: as Nekrasov expressed it,

> Golden, golden
> The people's heart.

Taking over from Pomyalovsky and Gleb Uspensky the work of moral—which inevitably meant political—exposure, Gorky moved towards the Marxist revolutionaries. A novel like *Foma Gordeev* (1898) showed his capacity for the kind of social analysis that Marxism encourages. Gorky understood very well the predicament and the temper of Foma, the son of a wealthy self-made Nizhny Novgorod merchant, as he appreciated the forces against which Foma had to contend, all the greed and despotism of his father's associates. In this second phase that establishes itself with *Foma Gordeev* and leads to *Mother* (1907), Gorky was bound to attract the notice of Lenin, who wrote to him fairly often between 1907 and 1916. Lenin told him that *Mother* was a 'necessary book':

> many workers took part in the revolutionary movement unconsciously, spontaneously, and now they are reading *Mother* with great benefit to themselves. . . .

Soviet critics have connected *Mother* with Lenin's famous tract on party organization, *What Is To Be Done?* Gorky helped, by his novel, to make the revolutionary workers conscious of immediate tasks. *Mother* is a weak-sided book, sentimental and declamatory; but as the first example of socialist realism it initiated a great deal.

This doctrine is to be discussed later.[2] It implies a relation between literature and politics which Lenin was already foreshadowing, if not actively preparing, in his idea of *partiynost'*, or 'party character'. Lenin assumed that literature could be used to serve the advance to socialism. Great works, even in the past, had their progressive side, but as human society became more aware of its destination, so literature would reflect more fully the aims striven for by the workers' party. Lenin himself, though he may have mocked the writers who did not want to become merely 'a little wheel and screw' in the general movement, read imaginative works, as Marx did, for more than their political use. It is said that he kept a volume of Tyutchev on his desk in the Kremlin, and Tyutchev was no soldier of the Revolution. But more impatient and cruder minds were soon to insist, once the Bolsheviks had triumphed, that literature must be mobilized and given its directives by the Central Committee. Even Mayakovsky, self-willed and original, came to demand that the party should padlock his lips after the day's work. This subordination of the writer to a civic purpose was nothing new in Russia. For generations criticism had been working towards that end. Tolstoy, recalling in 1901 the kind of criticism—'disinterested and belonging to no party'—that Arnold had stood for, could find little of it around him. And so eventually the dictatorship of the proletariat extended as if by right to literature. The Russian intellectual who felt guilty before the people, as so often he did, had no faith in the authority of his own conscience. Gorky indeed was more robust and the pangs of alienation did not touch him. The choice between direction and responsibility to himself hardly became real until he revisited the Soviet Union in 1928 and afterwards settled there. Ten years before he had repudiated Bolshevik policy. Now there were many inducements to accept the regime. He made his concession, perhaps even disguising it from himself. He would serve the Soviet cause, at a time when its enemies were becoming more active. During the last years (1928–36) Gorky as propagandist and literary guide was being led imperceptibly by the manipulators.

We have to consider less his predicament than the quality of his work, before and after 1917. Nothing he ever wrote had so powerful an influence as *Mother* or was more widely imitated. Gorky set himself to depict a 'hero of his time', the revolutionary Pavel Vlasov, who should also be a hero of the future. With Vlasov stands his loyal and courageous mother Nilovna. These long-consecrated images of the son who gives his life for mankind and the mother who blesses him (and here continues the work) raise the theme to the status almost of religious myth. From the opening scene in which the workers run out 'like scared cockroaches' to the sound of the factory hooter at dawn, and after the day's grinding labour are turned out like so much slag, the agitational purpose never drops. In the manner of Chernyshevsky's *What Is To Be Done?* this book is exemplary and didactic. What Rakhmetov in Chernyshevsky's novel meant to the revolutionary circles of the 1860's, Pavel Vlasov was to a still wider audience. Voroshilov when celebrating Gorky's completion of forty years as a writer called *Mother* 'the autobiography of the working class'. It is one of those books which, like *Uncle Tom's Cabin*, has a success much beyond its intrinsic merit.

The best of Gorky is not to be found here. *Mother* describes working-class life in Nizhny Novgorod from first-hand knowledge but it idealizes too freely the characters of Pavel and Nilovna. Gorky had a double vision, sober enough in detailing the present, but always ready to see miracles in the future. Great Romantics like Wordsworth, Keats or Baudelaire convince by their truthfulness. Gorky has a way of going soft at the centre. In this he resembles that other celebrant of sheer living and desperate action, Hemingway. The question with Gorky always comes down to the reliability of his writing. Realism, as Pasternak says in the essay on Chopin, means 'the highest degree of precision in a writer'. Stock romanticism works at a lower level.

Gorky's most notable work is that which deals directly with his life, whether in the three famous volumes of auto-biography—*Childhood* (1913), *Among People* (1918), *My Universities* (1923)—or in his incomparable memoirs of Tolstoy, Chekhov, Andreev and Korolenko. From the years of hardship and vagrancy he learned more about Russia in its length and breadth than anyone since Leskov. It happened that 1913 was a rich year for autobiography,

straight or fictional. James, Lawrence and Proust as well
as Gorky started on it at that time, to be followed a year
later by Joyce. But Gorky showed no interest in their
common theme—'the artist as a young man' or a child.
He wanted to expose the darkness and brutality which had
surrounded his own beginnings:

> Recalling those crass abominations of savage Russian
> life at moments I ask myself: are they worth speaking of?
> And with renewed conviction I tell myself they are, for
> this is the living and vile truth, it has not perished to this
> day. It is a truth that must be studied down to the roots,
> so that by the roots one may tear it out from memory,
> from the heart of man, from all our oppressive and
> shameful life.

> (*Childhood*, xii)

Alyosha Peshkov in *Childhood* may resemble Paul Morel in
Sons and Lovers at a particular moment, as when Walter
Morel beats his wife in a drunken fury or the Kashirins are
brawling, and the sensitive child in each case feels shame
for the grown-ups. Yet Gorky's interest goes outward:
Alyosha has no unique problem, no sense of a special
vocation. His one aim is to make everyone free. So he
seems more of a conscience than a consciousness. Compare
him with Irtenev in Tolstoy's *Childhood* or the Arsenev of
Bunin's autobiographical story, and the difference is plain.
Self-knowledge matters less to Gorky than the revelation
of social wrong:

> ... I am not telling about myself but about that narrow
> and suffocating circle of painful impressions which made
> and still to this day makes the life of an ordinary Russian.

> (ii)

Alyosha, virtually an orphan from the age of four when
he goes to live with his grandparents, meets in them at
once the Russian past and the new era. His grandmother
(after whom he meant originally to name the book) still
kept fresh the medieval lore of folk-tale and miracle: she

had much in common with the mother of Bazarov though
one was a squire's daughter and one a lacemaker. Gorky
writes:

> I very soon understood that my grandfather and grand-
> mother each had their own God.
>
> (vii)

And it is the grandfather's God—jealous and punitive like
that of the puritan in early capitalist days—which belongs
to the modern scene. Grandmother's God is fated to disappear with the patriarchal village.

> Her God was with her all day, she even spoke of him
> to the animals. It was clear to me that everything sub-
> mitted to this God easily and humbly: men, dogs, birds,
> bees and plants: He was uniformly good, uniformly
> near to everything upon earth.
>
> (*Ib.*)

But in the upheaval that enabled Vasily Kashirin, once
a haulier of barges, to acquire several dye-works, such
gentleness seemed remote. Thus the grandparents enacted
before Alyosha's eyes the developing drama of the age.
The book's title refers to the childhood of capitalism no
less than of Alyosha. And every character is there for
epreserntative value—the young workman killed by an
excessive burden, the blind foreman turned out to beg, the
misunderstood chemist with his invariable tag 'Good show'.
Like Saltykov-Shchedrin or Pomyalovsky, the author of
Childhood knew he was furnishing evidence for the pros-
ecution.

It was Leskov who made possible the rendering of this
story. In description Gorky is often laboured and weak;
his strength lay in the mimicry of voices, the exact notation
of a personal or a local idiom. He could catch the rhythmic
intonation used by his grandmother; the testy, abrupt and
sententious speech of his grandfather; or the meagre but
apt comments of the awkward chemist. This had been
Leskov's faculty, to present images not plastically but

through the ear. What Gorky wrote of Leskov in 1923 can be applied to his own work:

> The people in his stories often talk about themselves, but their speech is so astonishingly alive, so right and convincing that they stand before you no less mysteriously palpable and physically distinct than characters from the books of Tolstoy. . . .

When Gorky's characters speak, their authenticity is in no doubt. If only he had trusted to this dramatic sense, as Leskov did—but Gorky also fidgeted over the visual effect which is too often grotesque:

> She was altogether green: her dress, and hat, and the face with a wart under the eye, even the tuft of hair on the wart was like grass. Dropping her lower lip she raised the upper one and looked at me with green teeth, covering her eyes with a hand in a fingerless black lace glove. . . .
>
> (xii)

And further:

> . . . Her eyes were sewn on to her face by invisible threads: rolling easily out of their bony sockets, they moved very nimbly, seeing and taking note of everything, raised up to the ceiling when she mentioned God, dropping to her cheeks if the talk became domestic. Her eyebrows seemed to have been cut out and somehow stuck on. . . .

Gorky is prone to a kind of forced Dickensian wit:

> . . . if he smiled his thick lips rode up his right cheek, and his little nose also went that way, like a dumpling on a plate.
>
> (x)

Time and again people are likened to pike, goats, cats, dogs, camels. Gorky's descriptions often dehumanize, so intent is he on making the impression vivid; but once his characters acquire speech we can tear out these crude illustrations.

Blok compared the grandmother with the old matriarch in Goncharov's last novel *The Precipice*, who is there to symbolize Russia. He felt that the contrast told entirely in Gorky's favour. Akulina Ivanovna dominates the book as though representing the imagination and heart of the Russian people. However, a real woman supplied the image, and *Childhood*, though it may have features in common with a folk-tale, was designed as a document. Three writers, according to Gorky, did most to form his attitude to life. Leskov has already been mentioned. From the other two, Pomyalovsky and Gleb Uspensky, he must have learned a good deal about social analysis. Their influence—and of course that of the Marxists—is to be seen in the way he presents his grandfather. Vasily Kashirin with his rabid devotion to property was a typical man of the era following Emancipation. Gorky understood very well the peasant turned employer in that time of violent economic change. He had written of Kashirin's more successful competitors in *Foma Gordeev*. More than once these new industrialists whom he had observed in Nizhny Novgorod came under his fascinated scrutiny. The most elaborate novel to deal with them is *The Artamonov Business* (1925).

Its action begins in 1863 when the stranger Ilya Artamonov, till lately a serf, pushes ahead of the churchgoers in a town fitly called Dryomov (Noddington). Fifty-four years will see the whole business through, from start to finish. Ilya builds his prison-like factory, a tower of Babel as it seems to the townspeople. It grows steadily and then, vaunting his strength and mastery, he bursts a blood-vessel when trying to lift a new boiler. His son Pyotr succeeds to the business. Pyotr remains all his life a clumsy *muzhik*, but Alexey, his cousin and partner, picks up the methods and philosophy of the rising capitalist class. The factory expands, and its workpeople turn hostile; the old domestic relations which reconciled them to the tyranny of Ilya have now gone; Pyotr loses his grip, he breaks out in debauchery. Meanwhile his elder son Ilya, who has inherited the grandfather's energy as well as his name, will have nothing to do with the family business. He becomes a revolutionary. October 1917 rings down the curtain. Pyotr, helpless and uncomprehending, ceases to struggle. As a boy he had helped to mark out the site for his father's factory. Three generations—one to build, one to maintain, and one to lose—comprised the whole life-cycle of Russian capitalism.

The facts are impressive and Gorky had long considered them. But his novel, even though founded on actuality and showing an imaginative sense of Pyotr's predicament, is too contrived. Gorky makes out a neat paradigm. At the beginning stands Ilya the founder in all his rude confidence like the folk hero Ilya of Murom; at the end Pyotr, now a helpless invalid, turns away from a world that no longer needs him. There is an expected climax when Tikhon Vyalov, the workman who has kept his peace for so long, denounces the evil that Pyotr Artamonov has done or permitted. In another scene before this Ilya the favourite son rejects everything that Pyotr stands for; and compared with the confrontations of *Fathers and Children* this scene lacks subtlety. In *Childhood*—written before the Revolution—Gorky had shown Bishop Chrysanth as a man of deep sympathy and understanding. But in this novel the good priest Gleb must necessarily leave the church, and Nikita the monastery. For all its general truth *The Artamonov Business* has to be judged a Soviet rather than a Russian novel. Tendency leaves no room for the unforeseen.

Blok said of Gorky in 1919 that fate had 'set him as mediator between the people and the intellectuals'. At that time Gorky was trying to get a working relation between Russian writers and the Soviet government. In different terms this problem had always been before him. Gorky opened a new chapter in Russian literature, and from the beginning he attracted and shocked by an unfamiliar tone, and a conception of life that some found brutal and others elevating. It was his misfortune that the first proletarian writer to win international fame should have been drawn early into politics. Gorky wrote best as the poet of his own experience, but the age would hardly allow him to abjure a public role. The legend of Maxim Gorky put on him responsibilities; and finally he became a dignitary, a guarantor of good intentions, a national hero—but no longer the man of letters alone with his conscience. Gorky had a generous and sensitive heart; he did much to help individuals, and much to ensure continuity. As a writer he was overestimated both at the beginning and at the end of his career. The man who had known both Tolstoy and Chekhov might seem in retrospect like the third member of a triumvirate. It was partly accident that framed this role for him, and no serious critic would rank him with Chekhov, still less with Tolstoy. He did not change the face of literature by his talent. Other causes were at work, and perhaps with or without Gorky the result would have been the same. The one fact beyond dispute is that nobody else could have written his best pages, the true story of Alyosha Peshkov.

12

The age of decadence

TWO years before his death Tolstoy wrote to Leonid
Andreev (1871–1919), who at that time enjoyed a reputation
second only to Gorky's, complaining about the faults of
'modern' or 'decadent' writing. He found it not serious
enough, straining for originality, executed with too little
care, and dependent upon fashion. All these charges
(although Tolstoy did not directly say so) can be brought
against Andreev himself. The first two are not easily dismissed in the case of Andrey Bely (1880–1943), though he
took almost extravagant pains over his style. Ivan Bunin
(1870–1953), who gained attention more slowly than
Andreev or Bely, is hardly a 'decadent' in Tolstoy's sense,
but beyond any doubt he closes a tradition, and it might be
said that his Nobel Prize of 1933 was a posthumous award
to classical Russian literature. Fyodor Sologub (1863–1927)
writes a beautiful limpid prose, but he ranked among the
'decadent' poets, and his sensibility belongs to the wider
European decadence. As for Alexey Remizov (1877–1957),
the second master of Russian 'ornamental' prose after
Bely, he exploited the rhythms and tones of popular speech
in an unprecedented way, but it can hardly be denied he
was very often a bookish writer. Sometimes in considering
the work of all these men one remembers what Turgenev
said of the Goncourts: 'their literature reeks of literature...'[1]

Leonid Andreev began—as did Bunin—under the imprint
of *Znanie*, a publishing house guided by Gorky. His first
collection of stories brought immediate fame to him in
1901, and with this fame he continued uncomfortably for
another seven years. At the beginning he took his place in

the school of humanitarian and progressive writers which *Znanie* encouraged. Tales like *Bargamot and Garaska* (1898), in which a constable brings home a drunken vagrant to celebrate Easter with him, or *Petka at the Summer Cottage* (1899), about an exploited child, add nothing to Russian literature except a few lightly shed tears. *Once There Lived* (1905), chronicling the last days of a merchant in hospital, had the approval of Tolstoy, which is not surprising, for it keeps very close to *The Death of Ivan Ilyich*. Tolstoy however thought the end, in which the dying merchant and his fellow-patient the deacon break into a lament for the lost joys of life, 'unnatural and unnecessary'. Andreev shared the horror of death that Tolstoy felt so profoundly; but whereas Tolstoy faced it always with the sanity of a great moral artist, Andreev deliberately played on the horror. This happens in the best of his Tolstoyan pieces, *The Story of Seven That Were Hanged* (1908). Five youthful terrorists —two of them women—have been condemned to death, along with an Estonian farm-hand who murdered his master, and a bandit who has taken at least three lives. Andreev brings out the barbarity and senselessness of the ordeal through which they must pass, and he does it in the spirit of Tolstoy and almost with Tolstoy's precision and seriousness. But what most interests him is the old obsession with death, now stealing upon seven tortured consciousnesses. He has adopted the method and view of Tolstoy, and submitted them to his own distortions. Even so the story achieves a kind of grandeur. Andreev had for once managed to simplify his art.

This cannot be said of *The Red Laugh* (1904) in which Andreev tried to imagine the 'madness and horror' of war. He was no Stephen Crane. The genuine horror of Garshin's *Four Days* or the madness of his *Red Flower* make all too clear the pretentiousness and wilful hysteria in Andreev's attempt. Blok once said that Andreev expressed more vividly than any other contemporary 'the tremor of our fateful time'. But although he sinned repeatedly by overstatement, Andreev was more than the opportunist and expert at sleight-of-hand that he looks today. As Gorky's memoir or Blok's notice at the time of his death will suggest, he had a certain tragic dignity. However, he seldom wrote from a real centre, and for this reason his gifts were soon blighted.

The excellence of Bunin—limited but undeniable, both in verse and prose—connects him with the classical past and particularly with the writers of his own region: Pushkin, Goncharov and Turgenev. As he explains in the auto-biographical *Life of Arsenev* (1928–33) Pushkin had been always a household name, as it were 'one of ourselves', and the poet of his own daily experience. It was for Bunin—more or less in the tradition of Goncharov—to keep alive that world of the old gentry a few years longer. He contemplated it from the beginning with the eyes of a man already dispossessed, delighting as a child in 'the poetry of forgotten highways', and later when he travelled the steppes in memories of the heroic past. To him the Ukraine appealed all the more since

> its life in history has long ago ended for always. There is only the past, the songs and legends about it—a kind of timelessness. This delights me most of all.
>
> (*The Life of Arsenev*, V, xxi)

Much of Bunin's writing, even before he went into exile, is valedictory. He developed the finest notation to seize the beauty of that rural Russia which his great predecessors in the novel had celebrated before him, and he was gifted with exceptionally keen senses. Bunin is primarily a pictorial writer, with a mastery of the set-piece: an old-fashioned cemetery in the summer noontide, a boy's last day in the woods one August before starting school, the lying-in-state of a friend last seen on the doorstep 'blinking at the evening sun and his cigarette'. He eventually became skilled at the prose poem in the manner of Turgenev's *Senilia*. All his work had consisted of impressions caught and fixed: there is a stillness about it, despite the suppleness and dexterity of his writing. The prose conveys to perfection that sensuous delight and ironic despair which made up his sensibility. No modern writer in Russian achieved a style so pure and felicitous; but it stands (like the Ukraine) in 'a kind of timelessness'. Now and again one is aware of manner. Prose can offend by being too impeccable.

The English reader probably knows him best by *The Gentleman from San Francisco* (1915) which Lawrence translated with S. S. Koteliansky. This short story resembles the work of Conrad in its pictorial density—the carefully wrought surface—and its inward desolation. He represents his world of the Atlantic liner and the hotel in Capri as desperate, false and heartless. The rich are simply inhabitants of hell, with those 'gigantic furnaces' below the dancing hall of the ship where

> couples turned in the waltz or writhed in the tango, while the music insistently, shamelessly, delightfully, with sadness entreated for one, only one thing, one and the same thing all the time.*

Bunin encounters the same horror in peasant life at home. *The Village* (1910) describes the savagery and torpor of the rural scene: words and deeds never correspond in this 'Russian music'; the people are accursed, without honour or occupation, shiftless, wasted by disease and worn out by poverty. The story abounds in nightmare images of this order:

> At the table a stout blind girl was sitting and with a large wooden spoon she scooped milk with crusts of bread from a bowl. The flies, like bees in a hive, buzzed about her, climbed over her lifeless face, then fell into the milk, but the blind girl, sitting upright like an effigy and fixing the whites of her eyes on the dusk, went on and on eating.

Here is the typical poor man's hut:

> . . . if you enter its dark half-unroofed porch you feel yourself on the threshold almost of a beast's den—it

* Trs. Lawrence and Koteliansky.

smells of snow, through the cracks of the roof you can
see a gloomy sky, the wind rustles the dung and brush-
wood pitched anyhow on the rafters: you fumble to find
the leaning wall and open the door to meet cold and
darkness, and in the darkness a little frozen window just
glimmering. Nobody can be seen but you guess: the man
is on a bench—his pipe glows like a little coal; his wife—
a subdued, silent and foolish woman—gently rocks a
squeaking cradle where a pale rickety infant, sleepy
with hunger, is swinging. The little children have crept
on to the barely warm stove and are telling each other
something in a whisper. In the foul straw under the
sleeping-planks a she-goat and a sucking pig—great
friends—stir restlessly. You are afraid to straighten in
case you hit your head on the ceiling. And you have no
more confidence in turning round: from the threshold to
the opposite wall is just five paces.

It was Gorky who had suggested this theme to Bunin, and
much of what Bunin sees in the Russian village Gorky
had seen too. But the realism here is utterly without
comfort. In *The Village* as in *Sukhodol*—'Drydale'—(1911),
the record of a declining noble family, the Khrushchevs,
Bunin sets himself merely to tell the stark and often terrible
facts. He has the impartiality of a French naturalist, the
same concern with exact appearances. Bunin could not
isolate himself from history: both these stories show an
awareness of social change; but the history he knows is
meaningless and sinister. The pessimism Turgenev had
tempered with liberal hopes and warmed with the glow of
Pushkin's faith in humanity came down to Bunin un-
qualified. A writer of the backward glance, he left as his
testament the exquisite, lyrical and at times self-admiring
Life of Arsenev. Bunin's touch cannot be recaptured: it was
lost with his death. There died with him the memory of an
ideal, which he had contrived to believe in long after its
natural term, and to perpetuate in excellent prose.

Like Bunin, Fyodor Sologub was also a poet. His novel

of 1907, known in translation as *The Little Demon*, though it should more accurately be called *The Petty Devil*, is a prime document of the Russian decadence. Beautifully controlled, in a deft and perspicuous style, Mirsky held it to be 'the most perfect Russian novel since the death of Dostoevsky'. It stands in the Dostoevsky tradition, and derives its general sense from a work like *Devils*. The action occurs in a small Russian town—'our town'—which is presented as Gogol and Dostoevsky had made it inevitable to see all such places. At the outset the parishioners are grouped talking after church:

> All were dressed in holiday clothes, they looked cheerfully at one another, and it seemed that in this town people lived in peace and friendship. And even cheerfully. But all this was appearance.

The story concerns one Peredonov, a grammar-school master who embodies the principle of absolute selfishness. He is even more abrupt than Bazarov, coarse, cruel, suspicious and a prey to superstition. Being unmarried he figures in the calculations of various women, though he has promised to marry his mistress Varvara once she can secure from the princess who is faintly interested in her a promise that he shall be made inspector. Peredonov is capable of every meanness. He loves to defile and deface:

> At supper they all got drunk, even the women. Volodin proposed they should further dirty the walls. Everyone was delighted; at once, before they had finished eating, they set to work and disported furiously. They spat on the wallpaper, smeared it with beer, threw against walls and ceiling paper-darts greased at the ends with butter, stuck on to the ceiling devils made of chewed bread. Then they thought of tearing strips from the wallpaper, betting on who could pull off the longest. . . .
>
> (v)

The consequence is that Peredonov's friend Volodin, the sheeplike woodwork master, having lost the game suddenly

begins to ask why he was born and to despair of his life.
The emotional key is Dostoevskian, and Sologub can match
his master in devising new lengths of human pettiness:
Peredonov eats a pound of raisins and blames the cook,
torments his pupils, denounces his colleagues, tries to get
the cat shaved. All his hopes are fixed on a letter from the
princess, which Varvara eventually persuades a friend to
forge for her. Peredonov begins to fear persecution at every
step: not only the cat haunts him, but now a small familiar
devil which he names *Nedotykomka* gives him no peace:

> The *Nedotykomka* ran under the chairs and into the
> corners and screamed. It was dirty, stinking, odious and
> terrible. Now beyond any doubt it was hostile to Pere-
> donov and rolled up straight to him. . . . And now it
> lived, to his terror and destruction, magic and manifold
> —it followed him, tricked and laughed at him—now
> rolling on the floor, now pretending to be a rag, a ribbon,
> a twig, a flag, a cloud, a dog, a pillar of dust in the street,
> and everywhere it crept and ran after Peredonov, tor-
> menting and wearing him out with its wavering dance.
>
> (xxv)

Peredonov goes mad by swift stages. He cuts out the eyes
of playing-card kings and queens which are mocking him,
and finally, after setting fire to the club, murders his friend
Volodin.

The delusions of Peredonov go back to Gogol's *Diary of
a Madman*, and he resembles another solitary maniac,
Iudushka Golovlyov, when he shuts himself in his bedroom
and, alone with his terror, writes denunciations not only
against people but playing cards. At one point mention is
made of Chekhov's story *The Man in a Case*, about a
schoolmaster who shielded himself from the world and
tyrannized a whole town with his prohibitions. Sologub
has not Chekhov's social purpose, and yet in depicting
Peredonov as the future inspector, always ready to denounce
and intimidate, he makes his own indirect comment on
Russian life.

Peredonov at one time visits all the notabilities in the town to scotch rumours which he believes are circulating about him. The device is taken from *Dead Souls* and Gogol's accent can be heard in all this episode. Thus the public prosecutor's house

> had an angry ill-natured look. The high roof leaned gloomily down over the windows which were pressed to the ground . . . The gates, enormous and heavy, higher than the house itself, as though designed to ward off hostile attacks, were continually shut. . . .
>
> (ix)

But the general aspect of the town, with its grey weather, wretched buildings, nettles and dirt, places it in Dostoevsky's world. If there are passages that indicate Gogol, the dominant tone and the sensibility belong to the post-Dostoevskian era. Peredonov's surliness and bestiality could only have been conceived after Dostoevsky:

> His feelings were dull, and his consciousness was a corrupting and deadening apparatus. All that reached his consciousness was turned into vileness and filth. It was the defects in things that caught his eye and delighted him. When he passed an erect and clean pillar, he wanted to twist or befoul it. He would laugh for joy whenever they smeared anything in his presence.
>
> (*Ib.*)

The *Nedotykomka* comes out of Dostoevsky's hell, seeming to exist half in Peredonov's delusion and half in reality. Sologub has a similar sense of the ridiculous and the events of his story lead to the expected 'scandal'. And he feels like Dostoevsky about children. In those oppressive streets

> Only the children, eternal unwearied vessels of God's joy upon earth, were alive, and ran, and played.
>
> (*Ib.*)

He understands very well the misery adults can cause to small boys like the pupils of Peredonov.

Dostoevsky often shows an erotic awareness by no means common among Russian writers of the nineteenth century. In this book the relations between the young woman Lyudmila and the schoolboy Sasha (who is at one time generally suspected of being a girl) delighted Blok by their innocent hedonism. But it is impossible not to see them as perverse when Lyudmila dresses her boy in various female costumes, and then pets his bare shoulders; or when she speaks of the pleasure in suffering. The merry Lyudmila is allowed to save both of them from disgrace. Avowedly pagan, wily and passionate, she is untouched by moral discriminations, and Sologub seems to intend her as life-affirming in the mean world of Peredonov. Yet the idyll is queered. Sologub speaks more than once of the way people degrade and exploit beauty. This can hardly have been his intention with Lyudmila and Sasha; but to him as to Dostoevsky innocence appeals most when it is exposed to lust and cruelty.

Blok once described the author of *The Petty Devil* as an 'ironic Russian Verlaine'. Sologub's novel is admirably written, grotesque, buoyant and horrifying. It states the case of Peredonov with a scrupulous rightness. The Joyce who wrote *Dubliners* had a similar care for scale and definition.

Bely's *Petersburg* (five times published in varying forms between 1911 and 1922) has become available once more to the English reader. This romance and its predecessor *The Silver Dove* (1910) worked between them a revolution in Russian prose, breaking the traditional moulds and founding a new system which Bely called 'symphonic'. He admired the 'asymmetrical baroque' style of Gogol's early Ukrainian stories, their rich sound-patterns and incantatory power. *The Silver Dove*, as Mochulsky says in his excellent monograph on Bely,[2] is a great deal of it pastiche: you can easily recognize as Mirgorod the village where a young poet Daryalsky meets the votaries of a mysterious orgiastic cult. It needed very great virtuosity to bring back this style into service. Bely has in fact lived his story through Gogol: the whole conception depends on Gogol's rhythms and phrases

to sustain it. In *Petersburg* innovations crowd every page.
To begin with, certain consonants are used to convey
particular sensations—*l* to evoke 'glitter' and 'brilliance',
or *p* a feeling of airlessness. They structure the names of
leading characters, and play through phrases describing
scenes in the city. 'The influence of bodily movements on
the architectonics of the phrase', Bely declared, 'was an
America discovered by me as a young man.' Galloping in
the fields he had found kinetic rhythms for his verse; and
this method he now gave to prose. The result is writing of
extraordinary elaboration, which extends to the typo-
graphy. Bely builds his prose consciously on the principle
that Blok had followed at this time in his poem 'The Steps
of the Commendatore', where, as Mochulsky has demonstrated, the entire orchestration issues from the three vowels
of its hero's name, Don Juan, *o, u* and *a* each having a
distinct value.[3]

When prose aims at such closeness of texture, stylistic
devices tend to break away from the main fabric. Mirsky
has described this as 'the declaration of independence of
the smaller unit'. Both *The Silver Dove* and *Petersburg*
preserve their unity through the broad musical design, which
is supported in each by an imaginative scheme of some
power. Daryalsky the poet, who abandons his delicate
Katya for the freckled peasant woman Matryona and is
finally murdered by the community of the 'Silver Dove',
makes a symbolic choice between the civilization of
Turgenev's ideal and the dark potentialities of the peasant
masses. Katya's grandmother the baroness becomes a
symbol for the decaying order:

> Even so do not you, old and dying Russia, proud and
> fixed in your greatness, daily, hourly in a thousand
> chanceries, government offices, palaces and manors
> perform these rituals—the rituals of a bygone age?
>
> (Ch. iii. 'Tea')

In the background there are burnings and peasant revolts.
Bely's fantasy touches the predicament of thinking Russians

at many points. Daryalsky knows that if he submits to the spell of Matryona he will be ruined. Yet he leaves the manor and plunges into the thick sensual murk of peasant life, to be rejected and doomed. *Petersburg*, set in 1905, is a meditation on Russian history. The two Ableukhovs, of Tatar descent, the father a prominent statesman, the son a revolutionary who has pledged himself in an unguarded moment to parricide, stand for the two poles of Russian life. The theme of frustrated tenderness between father and son is personal (it recurs for example in the autobiography *Kotik Letaev*, 1922), but here a public significance has been added to it. The nihilism of these two Tatars is destroying Russia. Ableukhov the elder lives in a world of pure geometry (like Bely's father the mathematician Bugaev); Ableukhov the younger brings a bomb into the house. Finally he sees himself as 'a pyramid, the summit of culture, which will collapse'. Petersburg is a spectral city: a mathematical point at the centre of tangents and circles; and Peter, the Bronze Horseman, whose revolutionary will created this stronghold of reaction, bulks there as more real than the troubled shades that surround him. At one time he comes down from his pedestal and climbs, clanking portentously, up the stairs to a revolutionary's garret. Here Bely has recaptured the sonorities of *The Bronze Horseman*, just as Gogol and Dostoevsky helped him to his evocation of a phantom St Petersburg. It is a tone poem which abounds in momentary glimpses—the endless 'prospects' drilled into space, the green canals, the mists blurring gold spires and palaces, the heavy caryatids on the mansions, the murky dome of St Isaac's Cathedral, and at the centre of all the Bronze Horseman proclaiming: 'I shall destroy— irrevocably.'

Bely's prose, rich in irony, with a keen sense of the ludicrous, makes this novel the supreme bravura piece in Russian literature. It is grotesque art—Gogol outdazzled, and, in spite of the serious burden, spells decadence. It has all the features of Alexandrian writing: the literary echoes, the massed detail, the fragility. Bely's art is ultimately inhuman: it deals with the surface, with what he calls somewhere 'a heap of objects'.

Alexey Remizov was described by Mirsky as 'the most naturally Slavophil of modern Russian writers'. A bookman and antiquary, he developed a wonderful ear for the spoken idiom in its full native vigour and irregular freedom. Pushkin had listened to the Moscow wafer-bakers; but neither they nor Remizov listened in their turn to Pushkin. The language that Remizov learned to write still ran like a clear tumbling spring from the primeval forest. He was able to combine erudition with spontaneity. A connection could still be made between the genius of Russian literature before Peter's day and living informal speech of Remizov's own. He found his way to the *skaz*, an unforced colloquial tale which is not so much written as written down. It must bear the unique impress of its narrator who reveals himself through the spoken word. After the Revolution this technique became very general. Babel, for instance, used it with effect in a story like *The Sin of Jesus*; so did Zoshchenko in his anecdotes of Petrograd life; so did the early Leonov, and many others.

The work of Remizov shows wide variety. He had begun writing before the Revolution. In 1907 Blok noted his stubborn efforts to attain a personal style and already saw promise in Remizov's 'light, vivid and acute dialogue'. In 1910 Blok recognized him as 'one of the most serious and profound writers in our time' who had learned to 'guide his rudder through the ocean of Russian speech'. The 'shadow of untruth' which lay over Andreev and other moderns was, he felt, something that Remizov feared and for him it would pass. Fantastic, erudite, solitary, Remizov is perhaps at his most serious in the years of war and revolution.

Only a few weeks before the October rising in 1917 he composed his *Lament for the Ruin of the Russian Land* which in its archaic solemnity derives from the twelfth-century *Lay of Igor's Campaign*. As Blok and Bely had done a little earlier in their poems on Russia, he acknowledges the tragic fate of his people who 'have not seen that

with faith has perished the life of Russia itself'. Remizov
feels a stranger in his own land, 'and this curse is my lot'.
Another kind of eloquence controls the stories of private
suffering in the war, collected under the name *Mara*
('Northern Lights') in 1922, and in another more varied
volume, *The Noises of the Town* (1921), which deals in part
with the miseries of Petrograd after the Revolution. Here
the tones are more subdued to the general dark horror of
those times. Now and again Remizov mounts a declamatory
passage; the lyrical impulse only waits an opportunity to
soar out as in the sketch *Fences* on the return of spring 'after
bestial winter'. The last fences have been stripped down for
firewood, and suddenly a view opens from Petrograd to the
sea:

> And no more feeling oppression, I walked lightly
> among the gardens.
> So I would have gone through all the land,
> every land from sea to sea.
> And other words rose from my heart
> blessèd,
> blessing the dream of man.

Remizov's feeling in these stories is tender, one would be
callous to call it sentimental. He sets down the uncomplain-
ing tale an old woman tells of her sons lost in the war and
her Lithuanian farm burnt by 'our own lads'; his neighbour
attempts suicide to make things easier for her schoolgirl
daughter; he is comforted by the stars shining purely far
beyond the filthy staircases and freezing garrets of Petrograd; he feels kinship with a blind Chinese beggar seen in
the city:

> My frozen brother, do you understand what the word
> is? You were taught from the cradle to honour the word
> and the book. The word here, like your famishing self,
> has no place.

13

Soviet writing: the creative start

Two witnesses above all to the state of literature in early Soviet years demand a hearing. One is Trotsky, whose *Literature and Revolution* came out in 1923. Although he considered the writer to be a camp-follower—'the place of art generally is in the baggage-train of the historical movement'—Trotsky had some feeling for literature. He saw plainly that a proletarian art was impossible, and turned instead to the 'fellow-travellers' (a term he invented). Trotsky could write with stinging sarcasm and he made some neat formulations. However, the politician's view on literature is necessarily impure. A critic no less trenchant than Trotsky but juster and more sensitive was Evgeny Zamyatin (1884–1937), himself a Bolshevik and known as a writer before the Revolution. He found a cogent image to express the situation under War Communism:

> ... we were all shut up together in a steel shell—dark, close and shrilling, it carried us into the unknown. In those seconds (or years) before death you had to do something, to settle down and live in the hurtling shell ... And all the writers that were left huddled close ...
>
> (*Alexander Blok*, 1921)

It was Gorky who supplied the occupants of that steel shell with the means of living.

By 1923, when the New Economic Policy was starting to revive a derelict Russia, Zamyatin could report on the development of what might fairly be called Soviet prose.[1]

Bunin and others were abroad—'willow-twigs' which could flourish 'even in a bottle of water'. The 'good old wooden plough' of realism still kept going as it had in the *Znanie* times. 'Special incubators' had failed to 'hatch out any proletarian literature'. Casting round for more hopeful alternatives Zamyatin was bound to notice the 'Serapion Brothers' who acknowledged him as their master though he could not regard them as a homogeneous school. One of these, Mikhail Zoshchenko (1895–1958), will be taken here, together with Ilya Ilf (1897–1937), Evgeny Petrov (1903–1942) and Yury Olesha (1899–1960), to represent the light satirical trend which set itself to examining the quality of Soviet life under NEP. Earlier still Boris Pilnyak (1894–1937?) had made his report on the years of confusion and famine. A single story, *The Childhood of Lyuvers*, revealed to Zamyatin the little-known Boris Pasternak, working by himself in the neglected field of syntax. 'Socialist realism' was soon to strangle all other plants, and already two of its practitioners in the Stalin period, Alexey Tolstoy (1883–1945) and Ilya Ehrenburg (b. 1891), were making their first steps, though with little idea then of the final destination. It will be necessary to consider Mikhail Sholokhov (b. 1905), perhaps the greatest talent at the service of the 'social command', and also Izaak Babel (1894–1941), the most individual of Soviet writers, apart from Zamyatin himself.

To begin, then, with Zamyatin. He had started solidly in the tradition of Remizov with *Tales of Provincial Life* (*Uezdnoe*) in 1913–15. Here the idiom is heavy with the soil, knotty, outlandish. But Zamyatin was not long detained by the old-time rural scene, nor did he bring to it the piety of Remizov and their common master Leskov. It was H. G. Wells of the scientific vision who appealed to Zamyatin the skilled engineer. He saw revolutionary change as the law of life, and to express the new era he demanded a new style—rapid, incisive, concentrated—such as he had found in O. Henry. This he made his own; it was also mastered by Babel. He insisted:

> not one secondary detail, not one superfluous trait: merely the essence, extract, synthesis, revealed to the eye

for the hundredth part of a second, while all the senses are drawn to a focus, compressed and sharpened . . .[2]

The reader must be alert and supply the rest. Zamyatin's own prose is pure energy—'the high voltage of every word'. The rhetoric soon to weigh down Soviet literature never troubled its course.

In 1920 Zamyatin, a heretic on principle, wrote the novel *We* which has never yet been published in the Soviet Union. Orwell knew it and for the Western reader *Nineteen Eighty-Four*, his own variation on *We*, is bound to obtrude on the earlier work. Zamyatin had described Wells's stories of the future as 'social pamphlets dressed up in the art form of a romance' with the aim of criticizing the present. *We* is set in the world of nine hundred years hence. The Single State now prevails; unlike Orwell's Oceania it has no rival power-blocs to contend with, and is shortly to send out the Integral, a rocket-ship designed for the subjection of other planets to the 'mathematically infallible happiness' known on earth. This happiness has been won by annihilating Hunger and Love. The blue-print of the Single State can be found in Dostoevsky's *Legend of the Grand Inquisitor*: its buildings are fashioned after the style of his 'crystal palace'. Orwell's Airstrip One seems to belong to that era of the Two Hundred Years' War preceding the Single State. D-503, the builder of the Integral, whose diary we read, falls into heresy like Winston Smith through a woman who revives in him the passional life; like Winston he gives her up; and like Winston he eventually conforms. The Thought Police have conditioned Winston until he can truly love Big Brother. D-503 submits to an operation which burns out his imaginative faculty, that 'last barricade on the road to happiness'. Now men have become perfect, even as machines are perfect.

The structure of *Nineteen Eighty-Four* is very close to that of Zamyatin's novel, which derives in part from Wells (the subject of two interesting appreciations by him), but takes from Dostoevsky its main principle—that of the right to irrationality. D-503 as a child had been disturbed by the root of minus one:

> I remember it so very distinctly: the bright sphere-hall, the hundreds of little boys' round heads, and Plyapa our mathematician. We called him Plyapa: he was by now pretty well worn and shaken loose, and when the man on duty put in the plug behind him, the loudspeaker always began 'Plya-plya-plya-tshshsh', and then came the lesson. Once Plyapa was telling us about irrational numbers and I remember weeping, striking my fists on the table and wailing 'I don't want $\sqrt{-1}$! Take $\sqrt{-1}$ out of me!'
>
> ('Note 8')

The Single State has almost eliminated the unreal root: 'Taylor's exercises' rhythmically performed by all 'numbers', hymns to the Single State, dreamless sleep, love by pink coupon—('about three hundred years ago our historic *Lex sexualis* was proclaimed: "Every number has the right to any other number as a sexual commodity" ')—and now only two Personal Hours a day are conceded by the Hour Scroll to human weakness. D-503 rejoices in all this mathematical precision; but he cannot rid himself of one imperfection, his 'shaggy paws'. The daring girl heretic, I-330, brings him to the Ancient House where you can still see the furniture of an unregenerate world—

> We passed through a room where stood little children's beds (children in that epoch were private property too)—

and where the 'snub-nosed asymmetrical features' of Pushkin 'smile just perceptibly' from a shelf at D-503. His 'shaggy paws' have betrayed him, and he is drawn back into the disorderly past, with its primitive lusts and jealousies. It is these that break down the Green Wall of glass surrounding the city when rebellious 'numbers' unite with the naked savages who still hide in the forest. D-503, cured at last by the Operation, reports that 'a temporary wall of high-voltage waves' has been improvised. The book ends with his fervent declaration:

And I hope we shall win. More than that, I am convinced we shall win. Because reason must.

Zamyatin had not hit on Doublethink and Newspeak, but Thought Control is nearly absolute in the Single State. And his 'numbers' have already acquired an Orwellian mode of thinking: the Benefactor and a common criminal may act the same, but one has a plus sign, the other a minus. In the old world a spy may have been a stinking weed, but now he becomes a 'lily of the valley'. Elections in the Single State leave no room for the unexpected. Before Stalin, the Benefactor is already anticipating Big Brother. But although the lines of Zamyatin's indictment lead straight to Orwell's, the quarter of a century between them makes itself felt. Orwell to write *Nineteen Eighty-Four* needed less prophetic insight than did Zamyatin who had nothing like the same evidence at hand. There is a stronger affirmation of hope in Zamyatin's story. Whereas Julia in *Nineteen Eighty-Four* has been made ugly and cynical by her re-education at the Ministry of Love, and stands finally like Winston a peevish ghost of herself, I-330 does not break down under torture. The note of disgust almost drowns Orwell's humanity. Winston wanted 'everyone to be corrupt to the bones'—it was 'not merely the love of one person but the animal instinct', he believed, that 'would tear the Party to pieces'. If Zamyatin likewise thinks that sexual passion will prove stronger than the 'instinct of unfreedom', he does so because a living energy runs all through the universe, and Revolution defeats Entropy. Orwell can see life only in the mindless proles, but Zamyatin trusts the intelligence, which is committed to 'the destruction of equilibrium, the pain of endless movement' ('Note 28'). As I-330 tells D-503, there is no 'final number', and there can be no 'final revolution': in both, the series is infinite.

Zamyatin left the Soviet Union in 1931. He had no hope of returning until it should be 'possible to serve great ideas in literature without servility to little men'. A decade before this he had warned against the habit of treating 'the Russian

demos like a child whose innocence must be guarded'. If all
heresy should be stamped out, he was afraid that Russian
literature 'would have no future but its past'. When his turn
came to be silenced, he went reluctantly into emigration.

Boris Pilnyak saw the Revolution with very different eyes
from Zamyatin. He followed it into village Russia, and his
first major work *The Bare Year* (1922) deals, like the *Tales
of Black Bread* (1923), with the confused scene outside the
capitals. Pilnyak had no less than Remizov a delight in the
almost vanishing past. His archaeologist in *The Bare Year*
witnessing an ancient midsummer rite comments:

> Somewhere there is Europe, Marx, scientific socialism,
> but here a thousand-year-old superstition has been pre-
> served.
>
> (Ch. iii. 'As seen by Natalya')

The Bolsheviks in their leather jackets cannot be kept out
of *The Bare Year* but Pilnyak's imagination lingers on the
monasteries now facing their twilight hour, on a family of
princes soon to be dispossessed, on the unchanging peasants
who declare

> We are for the Bolsheviks, for Soviets, so that things
> may be our way, Russian style.
>
> ('Conclusion: Conversations')

At one point it is conceded that a factory brought to life in
1919, the year of famine and anarchy, may be 'a poem one
hundred times more splendid than the resurrection of
Lazarus'. Yet Pilnyak hoped for a return to the seventeenth
century and to that old 'wooden Russia' against which
Peter the Great had laid his axe. The Revolution for him was
a fable; it was a peasant's one day of revelry in a working
month:

> Russia has been drunk for five years—glorious years.
> Now she goes back to the daily round
>
> (*Black Bread*)

By a deliberately poetic style Pilnyak enhances the

fabulous quality of those years. As Zamyatin observed, he was 'evidently sown by Bely' though he had also, on his own admission, served apprentice to Remizov. From Bely he learned all the arts of elaboration which connect *The Bare Year* with *Petersburg*: the use of *leitmotivs* and recurring images (the smell of wormwood; bells crashing to the ground in *Mahogany*, 1929); the device of montage; the typographical oddities. Pilnyak's writing is wayward and mannered, yet a genuine personal vision shows through it. The years of hunger and bewilderment, when 'life was simplified marvellously to a matter of potatoes'; when 'a third of Russia was burning the spill', and the cherished green paraffin-lamp of the intellectual had gone out; when the nuns still sheltered in corners of their convents, and anarchists set up their communes in manor-houses; when crawling trains brought the townspeople to barter for food with the peasants: these 'Varangian times' found their chronicler in Pilnyak. He lived on to see the 'daily round' obliterate all memory of the five years' riot. In *Mahogany*, his last work of genuine inspiration, a gang of outdated revolutionaries huddle for warmth in a brick-kiln. Their leader is 'a holy innocent of Russia for the cause of justice, a beadsman for the world and for communism'. People recognized him in the town as

> one of those through whose mouths truth has utterance and who for truth's sake are prepared to die.

The holy innocent of today is a desperate alcoholic, 'cast out by the revolution, yet the revolution had formed him'. So Pilnyak dignifies the present by appealing to the traditions of pre-Petrine Russia. He invokes the old popular attitudes that look on the outcast with a compassionate awe.

Mahogany proved a stumbling-block: in 1929 Pilnyak was framed with Zamyatin. He revised his story and put it into a 'construction' novel, *The Volga Falls to the Caspian Sea*, probably his best-known work in English translation. But these efforts to conform did not save him from being destroyed in the purge.

The civil war (soon to become one of the central themes in Soviet writing) brought a moral chaos which demanded a style other than Pilnyak's to render it. This new accent was first heard in the stories of Babel, collected under the name of *Red Cavalry* (1926). The book contains some three dozen sketches, the longest hardly exceeding the slightest of Chekhov's pieces. Each records a moment in the campaign when some terrible and unprecedented insight is forced on the narrator. He cannot shoot a comrade dying in agony; or he has to gain the respect of the Cossacks among whom, a spectacled Jew, he is serving, by a show of brutality (*My First Goose*); or the young locksmith, his squadron commander, exposes him as a man 'trying to live without enemies' (*Argamak*). These experiences Babel narrates with a pitiless economy. His master was Maupassant, and he also admired Kipling. By constant reduction he made the essentials stand out in hard, precise images:

> More rain fell. Dead mice were floating along the roads, Autumn laid an ambush around our hearts, and the trees, naked corpses set upright on both legs, swayed at the cross-roads.

Two men have to save themselves in retreat, sharing a horse:

> . . . the morning seeped over us, as chloroform seeps over a hospital table.
> 'You married, Lyutov?' Volkov suddenly asked.
> 'Wife left me,' I answered and I dozed for a few moments and dreamed I was sleeping in a bed.
> Silence.
> Our horse stumbles.
> 'The mare will be all in after a couple of versts,' says Volkov sitting behind.
> Silence.
> 'We've lost the campaign,' mutters Volkov and snores.
> 'Yes,' I say.

> (*Zamoste*)

Babel learned to do without comment. Another story, *The Death of Dolgushov*, ends with his driver offering an apple to the narrator, whose cowardice has alienated his best friend:

> 'Eat it,' he said to me, 'do eat it.'

An earlier version had been more explicit:

> And I accepted the alms from Grishchuk that simple man, and I ate the apple in grief and reverence.

Babel worked very hard to overcome the pathetic strain (which persisted in Remizov). His own sensibility, as the tales of Odessa life make plain, was richly comic, even bizarrely so. But he set himself to expunge and shorten till he could attain a pure, cold outline. ('Only a genius can use two adjectives.') Babel's prose, seldom releasing more than ten words to a sentence, matches even Pushkin's for laconism; and it exactly answers to Zamyatin's specification. He gains his effect by trusting in the image presented for itself, and in rapid shifts of perspective.

War, as Stendhal and Tolstoy had shown, is a desperate muddle. Babel's own feelings were sharp and confused: so he penetrated the confusion by intensifying the sharpness. At the end of his career in 1934 he called himself, half mockingly, 'a master of the genre of silence'. He had indeed learnt what few Soviet writers were to understand, the art of leaving things unsaid. 'Let a noun live by itself, in its simplicity', unless you can find, as Babel so often does, the 'accurate simile' which reverberates in the silence.[3]

Sholokhov is a Soviet writer in another meaning of the term than Babel. He began to work when the Soviet power had established itself, and his acceptance of that power simplified the issues for him. Thus where Babel had seen the Cossacks and the civil war in flashes of half-bewildered intuition, Sholokhov could face steadily the whole sweep of history in motion over a wide landscape. His titles— *The Quiet Don*, *Virgin Soil Upturned*, *They Fought For Their Country*—promise amplitude and epic confidence. The first of these novels (1928–40) is a genuine epic both in scale and substance. It takes example from *War and Peace*, with Tolstoyan breadth and ease and sometimes Tolstoyan feeling, but it moves often with the fixity of *Resurrection*. Sholokhov understands the Don and its people with every pore of his body; knows intimately the voices, the tread, and especially the smell peculiar to Cossack men and women; and is a patriot of their soil. ' "In foreign lands," Grigory Melekhov tells himself, "both the earth and the grasses smell differently." How many times in Poland, the Ukraine or the Crimea had he rubbed in his palms a buish-green stalk of wormwood, sniffed it and yearningly tholught, "No, it's not the same"?' The images of Sholokhov's book, his frequent similes, all belong to the native scene: Aksinia winds herself about Grigory 'like the hops about an oak'; down the ranks of soldiers there runs 'a murmur, as though over a field of ripening dark buck-wheat a breeze passed playfully'; a soldier's face is 'greyish and dull, like a September field in stubble'.

The opening parts of Sholokhov's narrative (I, i, ii) put one in mind sometimes of Thomas Hardy: they stress the realities of rustic life, the necessary round that must go on whatever the human heart may feel. Thus when Natalya comes back home after Grigory's desertion, her father has been contending with another and more immediate mis-fortune: the best broodmare gored by a beast's horn. The two disasters have equal place. At the beginning Sholokhov establishes the order unchanged through the centuries— the watering of horses, ferrying, fishing and laundering which involve men and women with the Don as it flows by. His narrative has a backward reach, into the pagan, instinctive past which also delighted Tolstoy when he found it surviving among the Cossacks. This primitive and complete world is soon to be shattered by war, revolution and anarchy. The trader and the revolutionary have already entered it, each an active dissolvent. The Don steppes, like Faulkner's South, retain a backward culture with its own stiff pride and an oppressive romance. All this is present in depth when the story unfolds, the brutal uncomprehending ways out of which the Cossacks are to be educated by the Bolshevik Party. (Davydov in *Virgin Soil Upturned*, a workman of pure Leninist scruple, has his precursors in the earlier novel.) So the Cossack is remade, or promises to be. His type in Sholokhov's novel, the wild, headlong, heroic Grigory, cannot unlearn his past, and is doomed to the fate of the politically incorrigible.

Tolstoy in *War and Peace* combines an openness of response with a dogmatic purpose. Sholokhov too in *The Quiet Don* accepts life for what it is, and sees the Cossack as ruthless, bigoted but somehow fine—a straight manifestation of the will to be, like Hadji Murat in Tolstoy's story and the unyielding thistle that recalled him. On this side Sholokhov's imagination moves with unregenerate ease, but there is a censor at work, in the conception of history that he obeys. Grigory Melekhov, spoilt for the traditional ways by his experience in war, tries to understand and to serve the new. He cannot align himself with progress for very long, but lurches from one grouping in civil war to another, until he has lost honour, home, family and sense of direction.

> Like the steppe burnt out by fires, Grigory's life had turned black. He had lost everything that was dear to his heart. All had been taken from him, and destroyed by pitiless death. Only his children remained. Yet still he clung frantically to the earth, as though his broken life really did represent something of value for himself and others. . . .

In tragedy there is no school answer. The event overwhelms: man has final mastery of himself but not of the situation. As a responsible Soviet author Sholokhov gave up the right to tragedy. He saw a plain issue in all the chaos and suffering: the future would exert its beneficent power and cancel the past. Sholokhov matches the frankness of his apprehension, his natural poet's eye with a rigidity of mind that reduces tragic complexity in the end to simple politics. This limitation does not altogether diminish the power of *The Quiet Don*; but it becomes much more evident in his novel of collectivization, *Virgin Soil Upturned* (1931).

We have still to examine the 'positive' trend in Soviet literature which derives from Gorky's *Mother*. But in the NEP period there was even more 'negative' writing when Zoshchenko, Olesha, Ilf and Petrov, raised on journalism as Chekhov had originally been, and faced with the same *meshchanstvo* or vulgarity in wide areas of Russian life, turned to free satire. This was the age of the *feuilleton*, with its half-dozen paragraphs playing around some absurdity or abuse. Zoshchenko who thrived on this art had impressed Zamyatin as being the only young man in Petrograd who

> has mastered unerringly popular speech and the form of the *skaz*

—the anecdote in character which had been perfected by Remizov. He caught the peculiar tones of conversation on the Soviet street-corner—those 'rapid, curt, staccato phrases' that Mayakovsky noted as characterizing the modern city,[4] and its often uncouth jargon. A soldier in the queue 'pushes unculturedly'; lemonade is brought on 'an intellectual tray'; somebody wears 'an international overcoat'; another declares, 'I have always sympathized with central convictions.' This kind of utterance, with its detritus of political terms, had already been heard in Blok's poem *The Twelve*. ('Keep revolutionary step! The tireless enemy does not sleep'.) Zoshchenko uses it teasingly to define the attitudes of a new society, to expose muddled thinking, ignorance and folly—'some comrades suppose that [ethics] is a Spanish swear-word'. His writing continues in another place and time the early work of Chekhov ('Antosha Chekhonte'), though the idiom is more elliptical, with all the mannerisms of careless talk. Zoshchenko has one less obvious affiliation. He wrote a 'Sixth Tale of Belkin' and stated in his preface:

Not only certain of Pushkin's subjects but also his manner, form, style, composition were instructive to me.

I have sometimes thought that with Pushkin perished the genuine popular line in Russian literature, which had begun with such marvellous brilliance and was replaced (in the second half of last century) by psychological prose, alien in its essence to the spirit of our people.

Zoshchenko's irony operates with the elegance and control he had learnt from Pushkin. It proved unacceptable to the authorities who were irked by his deep-seated habit of disrespect. In the fulness of time Zhdanov denounced him as 'a literary slum-rat' and his career was finished.

Ilf and Petrov, with a very similar touch to Zoshchenko's, moved on from the *feuilleton* to the full-scale picaresque novel in *Twelve Chairs* (1928) and *The Golden Calf* (1931). These two journalists, both from Odessa, formed a single author in whom Ilf's structural sense and exactness of phrase served perhaps to control the exuberant dialogue and expansive views of Petrov. Their collaboration was wonderfully harmonious, and the two novels have a quality of self-delight so that you are aware of the dialogue of discovery that must have gone on during their composition. They owe much to Gogol—what Russian satire doesn't?— and something to Saltykov-Shchedrin. *Twelve Chairs* in particular recalls the manner of Shchedrin's *A Modern Idyll*. But the basic idea—of a hunt through Russia after twelve chairs, one of which contains a cache of diamonds— links the book with *Dead Souls*. The chairs, as Petrov afterwards declared, were soon recognized by them as 'a device for exhibiting life', exactly as Chichikov's mission had been. Once the ex-aristocrat, now a registrar of births, marriages and deaths, is joined in his quest for the chairs by that son of a former Turkish subject, Ostap Bender, the 'great entrepreneur', an inventiveness second only to Gogol's makes itself felt throughout this novel and its more closely designed sequel. Bender soon demanded the major role for

himself, and though killed by his accomplice at the end of the
first novel had to be resurrected in order to 'command the
parade' in the second. The satire lies partly in the con-
ceiving of absurd cases—an underground Soviet millionaire,
for instance, who is afraid to spend any of his wealth, or a
priest who dreams night and day of having his own candle
factory, or an undertaker's shop under the name of 'You're
Welcome' (*Milosti prosim*). It rises to real imaginative
power in certain scenes, as when Father Fyodor smashes
up the wrong set of chairs, for which he has sacrificed
everything, on the stormy beach, or when Ostap Bender,
at the end of his career, is plundered of all his portable
treasure by the Roumanians, and undeterred crosses the
Dniester into that Soviet territory of which he had just
taken farewell so movingly. But the excellence of Ilf and
Petrov, as of Gogol, shows above all in their language.
Ostap Bender, like all notable impostors in literature, never
fails for the surprising word. He creates vistas and trans-
forms every situation. His accomplice becomes at a stroke
'a giant of thought, the father of Russian democracy';
Bender is the perfect salesman, knowing what is done 'in
Europe and the best houses of Philadelphia', and raising
his glass 'to mass enlightenment and the irrigation of
Uzbekistan'. This creative energy deserts him only, and
then one feels against the authors' own inclination, when
he is confronted at the very end with a Soviet order that
regards him as meaningless. Till then he has improvised
his own meaning always with distinction. Amid the small
cheats, disguised reactionaries and routineers of the NEP
world Ostap Bender alone has a commanding intelligence
and the lucidity of perfect unscrupulousness. He is finally
degraded because, in a contest between him and the Soviet
State, Ilf and Petrov desired the latter should win. Their
satire was directed at a mentality that Communism aimed
to stamp out. They show absolutely no respect for the past:
all bourgeois and all priests, Orthodox or Catholic, are in
their eyes absurd and grasping. Ilf and Petrov belong to the
'twenties, the debunking decade, and to its most youthfully

critical society. Their high spirits overflow in an extrava-
ganza of detail, as they sweep up all the litter of a broken
world. No writers more freely invented placards, notices,
proclamations, inscriptions, from the 'No trousers' sign in
a clothes shop to the endless rubber stamps designed for the
Director of 'Hercules'. Their capacity for verbal nonsense
is infinite. Ostap Bender even uses a typewriter which has
a 'Turkish accent' through the loss of one important vowel.
Gogol lies at the back of all this, but the mere derivation
tells only half the story. Perhaps Ilf and Petrov wrote with
such irrepressible gaiety because at that time young Soviet
authors genuinely travelled light.

One more of this school has already been mentioned—
Yury Olesha, the author of *Envy* (1927). Both in Odessa
and Moscow he was acquainted with Ilf: they worked
together in 1924 on the same newspaper. Olesha's novel,
written with a grace and care for design that recalls the work
of Sologub, deals also with the transitional era. But Nikolay
Kavalerov, the victim of envy, presents a tragically absurd
case, unsuited to the boisterous style of Ilf and Petrov.
In the first half of the novel Kavalerov himself explains
why he hates his benefactor Andrey Babichev, the captain
of Soviet industry who plans an immense restaurant, 'The
Quarter Rouble'. 'He sings every morning in the lavatory.'
These are the opening words of the novel. Babichev
functions splendidly, working at high pressure, indefatigable and kind-hearted—he has brought Kavalerov into his
home after finding him drunk in the road. And Kavalerov
loathes him with an impotent fury. Babichev has a scanda-
lous brother Ivan whom Kavalerov first meets carrying a
pillow—the symbol for Ivan of the personal life which is
being destroyed by the Soviet system. Ivan tells him that all
the old private emotions are dying. He wants to shake the
dim electric light bulb into one feverish glare before it goes
out for ever. In Kavalerov he sees 'a clot of envy from a
doomed epoch'. He describes, very much in the spirit of
Dostoevsky's underground man, his ambition to do some
outrage on the new life from which he is excluded, just as in

childhood he had once scratched a little girl at a party and torn her dress. 'At that moment I loved this little girl more than life, I bowed down to her—and hated her with my whole strength.' So Ivan and Kavalerov feel towards the new people—the active if slightly philistine Andrey Babichev, the footballer Volodya whom he has taken as his son, and Ivan's own daughter Valya who has deserted to the enemy. Kavalerov has more than one tantalizing view of this girl for ever inaccessible to him, and finally he lurches into the embraces of the blowzy widow with whom he lodges. The story ends in the complete degradation of both rebels: Ivan's 'last parade' of the passions has been a fiasco.

Envy is beautifully written. Olesha has a fine eye for detail: he notices, after a rain shower, the little boy in a window who catches the sun with a fragment of looking glass; he watches a seed that hangs for a moment on a little girl's lip. This was virtually the first novel to touch on the theme of industrialization, and it does so with Chekhovian delicacy and justice. Olesha values the new life, and at the same time he understands the frustration of the last 'superfluous man'.

'It is very hard for me to find heroes,' Ivan complained. 'There are no heroes.' In the next phase of Soviet literature the difficulty no longer existed. The novel was given up wholly to the depiction of 'Soviet man', the hero of factory and collective farm.

Socialist realism

WITHIN a dozen years from the Revolution the hopes of
Soviet literature had been cruelly deceived. It was no longer
men like Zamyatin, Pilnyak or Babel who stood in the
public eye; and while some writers of talent—Sholokhov,
Ilf and Petrov notably—continued to produce interesting
work, a new conformity had arisen. The *émigrés* now
seemed very far away except those who had returned to
sink their talents in the collective pool. No other term
than a 'collective pool' can express what Soviet literature
was becoming. The traditional keen dispute between two
philosophies, two ways of feeling, to which the Revolution
seemed at first merely to have given a new urgency, after a
few years ceased within the Soviet Union. The opposition
was silenced at home. Literature had capitulated to the
State; and those who ran the State were ignorant of Burke's
discovery that 'our antagonist is our helper'.

Something has already been said about Lenin's insistence
that literature should be committed, that it should have
'party character' (*partiynost'*)[1]. The demand may seem
natural enough in a time of revolution and civil war, when
few writers preserve their lucidity and inner strength. But
even among those who want to ensure this commitment
some will proceed more gently than others. Trotsky, for
instance, warned against rash interference:

> Art must take its own road and on its own feet. The
> methods of Marxism are not the methods of art ... The
> province of art is not one where the party is called upon
> to dictate.[2]

However, by stages the party imposed its will on art as on

everything else. In 1934 at the First All-Union Congress of
Soviet Writers the government, which had brought them all
into a single organization, told the writers what it expected.
A. A. Zhdanov in the name of the Central Committee
exhorted them to 'create works of high mastery, and
profound ideological and artistic content'. He recom-
mended to his hearers 'the method of socialist realism'.
Like D-503 in Zamyatin's fantasy, writers who wished to
continue must submit to the Operation—and lose their
identity. Some made the choice willingly, from a sense of
public duty as yet unshaken by the purges—these were to
follow. Others like Babel elected 'the genre of silence'. To
some who supported fervently the government's drive to
'overtake and surpass' the industrial West, the new 'method'
in art may have seemed attractive and right. It was to prevail
for the best part of three decades, and still overhangs
Russian literature, ready to roll back and crush the shoots
that have lately emerged.

In choosing the name its sponsors could point to the
long tradition of Russian realism. This term, ever since it
appeared in the 1850's, has given trouble enough. But we
have seen that the Russian novel (and for that matter
Russian poetry) showed an unusually firm sense of man in
society. If 'realism' means the kind of complex awareness
that feels a moment in history as something unique and
intimate, then the Russian novel had grown up with
realism. The greatest things in Russian literature are indeed
realist to the extent of enlarging the definition. But whatever
Soviet writers may have supposed they were doing to build
on the classical heritage, in fact they were deluding themselves. 'Socialist realism' works in a different way from the
so-called 'critical realism' of the past. It is true that Soviet
writers study and imitate Pushkin, Goncharov, Turgenev
and Tolstoy. But what they derive from their great predecessors affects only the surface. The rendering may look
similar, as in historical novels which trail after *War and
Peace*; but you cannot have a living relationship with the
past unless you engage with it unreservedly. The encounter

must be searching on your side as well. Soviet novelists do
not risk their own assumptions when they resort to Pushkin
or Tolstoy. And so past writers, since they do not disturb,
lose their essential meaning.

In his speech Zhdanov called upon men of letters (re-
named by Stalin 'engineers of human souls') to 'depict
reality in its revolutionary development'. Their work, that
is to say, should combine the most painstaking realism
with heroic fantasy; should detail the present (soon to be
left behind) and celebrate the future, thus pre-empting the
unknowable. An art at once so restricted and so indeter-
minate, part document and part dream and all propaganda,
came into the world broken-backed. When a novel has to
be revised each time an 'incorrect' policy is discarded it
loses face and forfeits the authority by which we at once
recognize a work of art. The Soviet writer, listening intently
to the 'social command', becomes deaf to the muse.

The Puritan imagination, it has been said, failed to realize
more than a single theme, the individual's quest of salvation, so that all its works seem variants rich and poor of
The Pilgrim's Progress. In much the same way, but more
disastrously, Soviet literature has imposed its own scheme
on experience. Those writers who followed the method of
socialist realism produced in essence, under all its varied
forms, the same novel. The scene might change from civil-
war battlefield to workshop or construction site, from
primeval forest to collective farm. But the perspective was
always the same, and every one of these novels expressed
the theme in the title of Nikolay Ostrovsky's famous story,
How the Steel was Forged (1932–4). Soviet literature under
the Five Year Plans showed how revolutionary cadres are
made that will transform the people, the landscape and the
mythology of Russia. Gorky had told the same congress
that Zhdanov instructed:

> As the essential hero of our books we ought to choose
> labour . . .

labour as creation. The interest now shifts from the

individual (Olesha's Ivan with his pillow) to collective man; civic passion becomes the deepest reality in life; heroism the natural mode. A novel like Chernyshevsky's *What Is To Be Done?* had pointed this way; Gorky's *Mother* was more directly responsible. In perhaps ninety-nine out of a hundred Soviet novels experience has been falsified, not everywhere and not consistently, but to such a degree that any 'thought adventure' becomes impossible. We have seen journalists at home hypnotized by the image they have made for themselves of the newspaper-reading public. When, as in the Soviet Union, a writer is forced to hear the criticisms of laymen and to take back his work for amendment, he can have no integrity as an artist. The collective judgement (however arrived at) is better than his own. Hence the predictability, the middle-brow tedium, of Soviet literature. Just recently there have been signs of an attempt to break away from party dictation. But earlier dissident novels like Dudintsev's *Not By Bread Alone* (1957) did nothing radical. The movement stayed all on the surface. Yet it is only from the deepest places that the imagination can proceed to work its own revolution.

Soviet fiction of the approved pattern has always set itself big tasks. There were the novels seeking to represent the civil war: Dimitry Furmanov's *Chapaev* (1923), which comes very close to a historical memoir; A. Serafimovich's *The Iron Torrent* (1924); Alexander Fadeev's *The Rout* (1926); Alexey Tolstoy's *The Road to Calvary* (1941). Perhaps the most original among these was one of the earliest: Vsevolod Ivanov's *Armoured Train* (1922). Then the period of industrialization and of the change to collective farming demanded its own literature: Leonid Leonov's *Soviet River* (*Sot'*: 1929); Fyodor Gladkov's *Cement* (1931); Sholokhov's *Virgin Soil Upturned* (1931), and many others. There were historical novels, like Alexey Tolstoy's *Peter the First* (1929–45), and the numerous works of Sergeev-Tsensky: the periods chosen had to allow the writer a fairly sure ideological footing, and it was his duty to foster the new Soviet patriotism. This naturally ran high in all novels of the officially named Great Fatherland War, 1941–5, the most ambitious of which is perhaps Ilya Ehrenburg's *The Storm* (1948), subsequently revised.

George Santayana once complained that most people have a *diplomatic* notion of things: they never see a face with the attention that Dickens gave.[3] Almost any page of Babel or Pasternak startles the reader by its acute personal vision—the wonder and the poignancy that only the unenlisted mind is able to feel. Rarely indeed do such moments occur in Soviet writing since 1930. It has suffered from the censorship imposed from without and more subtly from within; and what was once a world literature soon became provincial and barren.

To show the difficulties that beset a writer who has a Soviet conscience we can take the last novel of Leonid Leonov, *The Russian Forest* (completed in 1953). Max Hayward said of this book:

> His most impressive 'feat' was the novel *Russian Forest*, written in the most difficult years preceding Stalin's death ... Impeccably 'socialist realist' in tone and structure, this novel yet manages to suggest by devious symbolism that human affairs and the fate of Russia are much more complex than the crude over-simplifications of official thought would ever follow.[4]

Leonov had demonstrated a quarter of a century earlier in *Sot'* that a Soviet novel need not refuse quite subtle moral discriminations. Originally a disciple of Dostoevsky, he was able to retain in the new conditions that respect for human difference which a novelist cannot work without. *The Russian Forest* still treats certain predicaments with a fine understanding. It enters into the misery of Vikhrov's wife whose upbringing has made her suspect until after years of devoted service as a nurse she is at last 'taken into the great good warmth':

> Recognition of being needed came at the moment when she had least counted on her efforts being noticed. This

was the right to one's own country which more fortunate
people receive with their mother's milk.

(IX, 4)

And at the same time Leonov chides Soviet youth for its
brave ignorance:

All the world's wisdom had come to Seryozha in ready
digested form—he did not have to labour on his own for
the elucidation of truth.

Leonov concludes that

The older generation, having proved by experience all
the misfortunes of social disorder, tried in every way to
save the next one from humiliating want, and also to insure
it for ever against all possible maladies of the spirit.

(IX, 5)

Vikhrov's young daughter Polya could not foresee the cruel
initiation of war that lay just ahead of her. She is what the
saddened woman from a past Polya could not understand
calls her, a 'girl from the provinces':

'. . . excuse me, from the periphery,' she corrected herself according to the fashion of the age which aimed at
levelling all citizens so that none should feel upset. . . .

'You don't know, my dear [the same woman tells
Polya] how fate is liable to deride our plans.'

She discusses the subject with Polya, and observes:

'. . . a person's youth lasts until the time when he first
utters this word "fate" in connection with himself.'

(I, 1)

Thus gently but persistently Leonov corrects the naïveté of
the provincial view, and it must be remembered that the
ideas which Sonya and her friend Varya expound so eagerly
—Varya 'as though at the same time she were writing in
chalk on a blackboard' (VIII, 1)—reflect those of the
society at large. It is not only children who have to learn that
the 'refined logic of prejudice' must give way to the 'clear
logic of life': as Polya discovered,

life is always wiser and more persuasive than any of the
fancies with which people from various motives try to
increase the beauty of truth or to heighten the deformity
of evil.

(I, 3)

The Russian Forest deals with the time-honoured theme of
illusion and reality.

Polya has to find not only herself but her lost father, the
much traduced Ivan Vikhrov. In recognizing that truth lies
with him rather than with the intriguing Gratsiansky she
chooses for her generation between two moralities. Vikhrov,
the peasant-born Professor of Forestry, is a character out of
Chernyshevsky, and not unlike Nikolay Gavrilovich himself with his innate uprightness, his charming pedantry and
his absolute devotion to an ideal. A 'just man' (*právednik*)
like Father Tuberozov, but finding his truth in science not
religion, he has already been encountered in Chekhov's
The Grasshopper. The virtues of Vikhrov are those long
cherished by the Russian intellectual: patient toil, simplicity
in his dealings with men, a high regard for duty, patriotism
and cleanness of life. For Vikhrov the Revolution meant this
last more than anything else: 'human cleanness', an end
to physical squalor and moral corruption (II, I). This
aspect of Vikhrov is endearing. So too is his attitude of
piety towards the Russian forest. The poet Osip Mandelshtam (1891–1938) once called the historian Klyuchevsky a
'good genius' and 'household spirit'[5]—Vikhrov's annual
opening lecture on forestry (quoted to the length of fifty
pages) breathes the spirit of Klyuchevsky.

He feels for the forest as though it were his own mother:

> When my eyes opened on the world, over me the forest
> was leaning . . . here lie the roots of my devotion to it,
> like that. . . .

(VI, 3)

('Like that' is a trying mannerism of Vikhrov's, to be compared with Davydov's 'fact' in *Virgin Soil Upturned*.) The
tutelary genius of the forest, old Kalina, imparted his

wisdom to Vikhrov in childhood, and the spring deep in
the forest where Kalina lived causes the boy an exaltation,
a mystical sense of having penetrated to the source of life
(II, 3). Vikhrov's intimacy with the forest has given him a
'master-light of all his seeing'; and this principle contends
throughout the book with civic responsibility which makes
him locate wisdom in the Kremlin. Leonov cannot avoid
showing Comsomol officials and Soviet diplomats as the
naivest of Russian youth might imagine them. When Varya
reminds Polya:

> You have a Comsomol card under your pillow ... think of
> it more often—it will teach you to accomplish great things.
>
> (VIII, 1)

does Leonov betray the least flicker of amusement? Hardly,
it would seem. The entire system of values behind that
comment is allowed to stand, just as a rather different one
is disclosed here:

> 'And so with deep satisfaction I thank you for your
> bread and kindness,' said Elena Pavlovna rising from the
> table with a courteous bow, as earlier shepherds had
> done, reapers, carpenters coming from distant parts, with
> the assured dignity that derives from knowing one's skill
> and the usefulness of the work done.
>
> (IX, 4)

Leonov has allowed himself to simplify in the opposition
between Vikhrov, all solid shy worth, and his unbelievable
adversary the ex-gentleman Gratsiansky. From the beginning Gratsiansky's final exposure never hangs in doubt, any
more than Vikhrov's final triumph. This simple Dickensian
scheme nearly ruins the novel. Now and again Leonov cannot
avoid the tedium of Soviet platitude and Soviet jargon:

> After the parade on Red Square [the locomotive-men]
> through their party organization turned to the govern-
> ment with a request for a supplementary burden in
> excess of the plan.
>
> (XI, 1)

This sentence is pasted on to the page in yellowing news-print. It needs to be translated into the only language a novelist can use, the direct words of experience. The trouble is not that we have to deal here with manners or conventions we don't understand. Simply the quickness has gone. And in *The Russian Forest* two voices alternate: the first genuine and sometimes moving, which seems to belong to the Russian forest, and is at its finest in describing the country and people under German occupation; the other flat, and often sentimental with its constant diminutives, that of a people encouraged to fall in love with a superior image of itself. Leonov as an intelligent man tries to guard against this tendency. But the Soviet novel cannot help being narcissistic. It knows too imperturbably what to admire.

Soviet literature has failed in spite of the vast human activities with which it deals. To extricate a whole nation from unwanted war; to raise a new citizen army; to repair and enlarge factories, and to dam rivers and plough the steppes; to alter the conditions of human life, with the hope of transforming the mind and capacities of man—such purposes would take a genuinely heroic literature to do them honour. But the heroic only has meaning when it is kept in scale—the scale provided by a free imagination aware of the failure that accompanies all success. In Soviet literature the imaginative scope of the previous age, the living sympathy, the verbal richness and the surprise have all shrunk away.

Light and air, of course, are returning. The language, debased by newspaper jargon and all the verbosity of over-insistent proof, does not lack the power to recover. But once the imagination tampers with its own deepest sources, there is no end to the falsification that ensues. Soviet literature mixes sincerity with a cynicism that it may often fail to recognize—the cynicism that puts forward expediency in the place of truth, without pausing to distinguish them. It has abolished the tragic sense, and so ceased to be a literature for grown minds.

Doctor Zhivago:
a novel in prose and verse

THIS is a poet's novel. It cannot be judged as socialist realism, or as an attempt to produce something like *War and Peace*. Pasternak tried earlier to get historical breadth in poems like *Nineteen Five* and *Lieutenant Schmidt*. The method of *Doctor Zhivago* (1957) remains poetic. Not only does it make use of verse forms in the final chapter, but the whole procedure, with melodrama, coincidence and symbolism to bear much of the meaning, recalls *Moby Dick* or *Ulysses* rather than the customary novel.[1] Pasternak has named metaphor the shorthand of genius. *Doctor Zhivago* is written largely in shorthand: it has the abrupt transitions of Pasternak's poetry, or of earlier prose pieces by him such as *Letters from Tula* (1918) or *Aerial Ways* (1924). The reader soon recognizes the part played by images like the candle in Pasha's room (III, 9–10) which suggested a memorable poem (No. 15, 'Winter Night'), and which is brought back to mind in the second Varykino episode when Lara addresses Yury as 'my bright candle'. Nor should we feel disturbed when Zhivago's corpse is laid out in the very room that Pasha had once inhabited, or when Lara arrives there after long years of absence to mourn him. The destinies of Lara, Yury and Pasha Antipov (later Strelnikov) cross mysteriously—an economy of design that helps to concentrate meaning. Even the 'complete' novel—*Anna Karenina*, for instance, or *Daniel Deronda*—has its analogies and returns, and does not deny itself some poetic devices (the wheeltapper, Mrs Glasher's diamonds). *Doctor Zhivago* follows on from the longer poems of Pasternak, which tried to relate moments of lyrical insight to large public events only here and there seizable as poetry. In the novel Pasternak found a more capacious form than narrative verse today offers. Poetry since the age of Pushkin has come to rely on the instant of divination giving an intensity to which the lyric is best suited. It aims at the power which Pasternak says never failed Tolstoy, the power to see things 'in their original freshness, newly, and as it were for the first time'. Tolstoy could sustain this vision through the multiple incidents of a novel. Pasternak also turned to the novel: Yury, we are told,

> had dreamed even from his schooldays of prose, a book of life-stories . . .
>
> (III, 2)

and towards this the poems he wrote were preliminary sketches. Only perhaps through the novel which is 'a book of life-stories'—and every life its own centre—can the lyrical impulse branch out into something like epic fulness. Pasternak notes that Verlaine brought into poetry the idiom of city streets hitherto confined to the novel and drama. His own verse had in the same way made contact with the novel, and to carry over the precision of verse into narrative prose was the next step. *Doctor Zhivago* can be broken down into, it may be, hundreds of separate lyric notations, as when the refugee party on arriving at Mikulitsin's feel the enormity of their intrusion:

> The sense of oppressiveness was communicated to the mare and foal, to the golden rays of the sun and the midges that wove round Elena Proklovna and settled upon her face and neck
>
> (VIII, 9)

or when, at the moment of losing Lara, Zhivago

> took in everything with tenfold acuteness. The surroundings now had a rare aspect of singularity, even the very air. An extraordinary compassion breathed from the winter evening, as from a witness sympathizing with it

all. As though there had never been twilight till then,
and evening came today for the first time to console the
bereaved man who had fallen into loneliness. As though
it was no mere encircling panorama of woods that stood,
with their backs to the horizon, on the hillocks around
him, but they had only just taken up their positions,
coming out of the earth to declare sympathy.

(XIV, 13)

Such passages are the substance of Zhivago's lyrics in
Chapter 17. Their 'rare aspect of singularity' can be called
Tolstoyan; but Pasternak has organized his work not like
Tolstoy the poet-novelist, but as a novelist-poet.

This means that we have to suspend our normal pre-
judices about fiction. Not only must we accept coincidence
and also rapid transitions—the fourth section of Chapter 4
ends with a train gathering speed, which then carries us into
the second autumn of war—but there is that odd sequel,
the poems of Yury Zhivago, presented as the last chapter.
Like Ivan Karamazov's 'poem' about the Grand Inquisitor,
they are what the book exists for: its essence and justification. Or at least the justification of Yury Zhivago,
proving his title to genius as the Legend of the Grand
Inquisitor proved Ivan's. The true life of Zhivago, its
profoundest meaning, must be sought in the poems. He is
most himself during those nights at Varykino when the
language of inspiration takes hold of him, and he comes
back from the experience 'happy, strong and calm' (XIV, 8).
In the words that Pasternak applied to Verlaine (and to
Blok and every realist of the arts) Zhivago too 'left a vivid
record of all he had lived through and seen'. The poems
cannot be detached from the novel, since they belong
specifically to Zhivago, and the novel provides a necessary
gloss on them. Nor can the novel be read without the
poems, which are a meditation on its events. Thus Pasternak
affirms that poetry and life, art and history, mean most in
their interplay. To separate 'the man who suffers' from 'the
mind which creates' was never his purpose.

The poems have the effect of ordering and relating the wayward and unsystematic career of Zhivago. By vocation a poet, who trains as a doctor to use his intuitive gifts, he fails in life. Deserting two wives, leaving his post as medical officer to the partisans, drinking and going to seed with undiminished self-regard ('The only live and vivid thing about you is that you lived in my day and knew me', XV, 7) —his conduct is enough to shock, equally, the modern Soviet reader and an intellectual of Chekhov's stamp, believing in austerity and self-control as the scientist's virtues. Zhivago has no will—unlike Liberius and Pasha Antipov. The Comsomol girl in Leonov's *Russian Forest* would not allow the notion of fate: 'there are only iron wills and necessity'. But Zhivago is a Christian hero, strong in his weakness, and the first of his poems ('Hamlet') accepts the bidding of fate:

> I love Thy resolute design
> And do consent to play this role.

Life for him, as for his uncle and mentor Vedenyapin, has to be sacrifice. He is not bothered with trying to 'remake life', as though it were an inert substance waiting to be kneaded (XI, 5). The poems inform us about an aspect of Zhivago his friends could not see: Zhivago, as his uncle would put it, 'in history'. When Yury wrote about Lara after she had gone her image in his poetry became something more remote from 'the living mother of Katenka'. In place of the actual agony and bleeding there appeared 'a broad serenity which raised the particular case to the generality of what is known to all' (XIV, 14). This is what happens to Zhivago in the poems: he must not be identified with Hamlet, still less with Christ. His uncle's new conception of Christianity had led to a new conception of art (III, 2). The poet—like Russia itself—must pass through the darkness of the grave to achieve resurrection.

By chance Leonid Pasternak illustrated Tolstoy's *Resurrection* when his son was a small boy.[2] The opening paragraph has a close bearing on what Boris Pasternak was to do in *Doctor Zhivago*. Tolstoy describes how urban man tries to suppress nature, but 'spring was spring even in the city':

> The sun warmed, the grass coming to life grew and showed green everywhere that it had not been scraped away, not only on the boulevard verges but also between flagstones, and birches, poplars, bird-cherry unfurled their sticky and scented leaves, the limes swelled their bursting buds: jackdaws, sparrows and doves with the joyfulness of spring were already preparing their nests, and flies buzzed by walls as the sun warmed them. Happy were plants and birds and insects and children. But men —fully grown men—did not cease to deceive and torment themselves and each other. Men took as holy and significant not this spring morning, not this beauty of God's world given for the welfare of all beings—a beauty disposing towards peace, harmony and love, but as holy and significant the things they had themselves plotted to dominate each other.

It is remarkable how Tolstoy in this paragraph sets the moral scale, the implicit values, for *Doctor Zhivago*. Pasternak's theme includes the self-deceit and mutual tortures of men, but always behind and above stands the 'beauty of God's world' which Yury celebrates in the midst of suffering, as does Lara when she has barely escaped from Komarovsky: on the path from the station which pilgrims have trodden she pauses to drink in

> the bewilderingly scented air of the expanse around her. It meant more to her than father or mother, was better than a beloved and wiser than a book. For one moment the purpose of life was again disclosed to Lara. She was here—she now came to see—so as to make sense of the wild fascination of life and to call everything by its name.
>
> (III, 7)

Nature has the primacy. There is a memorable scene in which Commissar Ginz, under a moonlit sky 'as astonishing as mercy or the gift of clairvoyance', harangues the people using 'measured clipped sounds'. His voice trespasses upon 'the hush of this bright sparkling fable' (V, 7). Again, Yury vexed and weary among the partisans turns to the sight he has always loved of the evening sun that penetrates the forest.

> At such moments he seemed to let through himself the columns of light. As though the gift of a living spirit flooded into his breast, intersected his whole being, and issued in a pair of wings from his shoulder-blades. . . . 'Lara!' closing his eyes he half-whispered or turned in thought to his whole life, to the whole of God's earth, to the whole sun-illumined expanse stretching before him.
>
> (XI, 7)

Neglected fields overrun with mice, railway trains derelict in the snow-drifts, ruined villages confess the human failure. 'Only nature stayed true to history.'

On the long railroad journey to Yuryatin they have halted for some while by a wrecked station. The sun

> as though in fidelity to the past continued to set in its former place, behind the old birchtree growing right against the window of the telegraph office.

Part of the room has survived, recording a lost human routine, with the wallpaper and stove, the framed inventory. All this has passed out of reach, but

> Sinking earthwards the sun exactly as before the disaster reached out to the tiles on the stove, kindled the coffee wallpaper with a brickish glow and on the wall it hung like a woman's wrap the shadow of birch twigs.
>
> (VII, 16)

Nature preserves the hope of continuity. Though the untended fields seem to Yury given up to the devil's mockery, 'God inhabits the forest'. There freedom and beauty have been restored.

In contrast men 'plot to dominate each other'. Pasternak as witness of his own time is compelled like every other

Russian to appraise the Revolution, its motives, its character and meaning. He continues the effort of Babel and Pilnyak to render it as immediate fact, to call revolution and civil war by their proper names. This is what poetry must do, ignoring the interpretations, Bolshevik or White, which are put upon the reality. To Pasternak it seems that men like Strelnikov and Liberius—indeed Lenin himself, 'a genius of self-limitation'—for all their devotion to the common good lack one saving gift. They do not allow for the unexpected. When Zhivago sheltering from the blizzard (the blizzard of Blok's *The Twelve*) reads those first Bolshevik decrees in their ruthless simplicity, like his father-in-law Gromeko he is carried away. But afterwards Gromeko says to him:

> Do you remember how unconditional it seemed, like nothing before? There was no gainsaying that down-rightness. But such things live in their original purity only in the heads of those who create them and then only on the first day of proclamation . . . This philosophy is alien to me. This government is against us.
>
> (VII, 26)

'Against us': 'we Gromekos', as he tells Yury, 'personally gave up the rage of acquisition a generation ago'. Gromeko like Yury's uncle has the candour and generosity which are in the true sense liberal virtues; and their way of thinking survives after the Revolution only in Zhivago and Lara: a freedom from 'the despotism of the phrase'. In that miraculous summer of 1917 a God had come down to earth

> and everyone went mad in his own way, and the life of each existed for itself, and not as an exemplary illustration to confirm the correctness of higher policies.
>
> (XIV, 14)

In Pasha Antipov (who becomes Strelnikov) is revealed the pathos of the dogmatic self-justifying mind. Those who take their own lives, Pasternak wrote in the *Autobiographical Sketch*, 'renounce their past, declare themselves bankrupt'. There can be no resurrection for Strelnikov.

The death of Zhivago himself is ignominious enough, struggling out of a crowded tramcar to die in the street. He has made 'a superhuman effort of will'—this man who appears to lack any will at all—because he needs air and freedom. The other passengers have shouted to him that the window cannot be undone. Meanwhile the old Swiss lady from Melyuzeyevo, toiling up the same street, has the promise of her escape out of Russia. Zhivago's death though 'in the street' also takes place 'in history'. It is a symbolic act. The crowd who resist and curse him cry out that the window to freedom must stay shut; the old lady receives her freedom by the caprice of government. Zhivago opposes the crowd who will not let him pass; he breaks free, only to die. And this manner of death is true to his whole life. When Lara mourns him she knows again the 'atmosphere of freedom and unconcern' which was peculiarly his. They had loved freely, and with the consent of 'the earth under them, the sky over their heads, the clouds and trees'. Always they had preserved 'the sense of their own relation to the whole picture' (XV, 15).

This sense of relation belongs peculiarly, as Lawrence has claimed, to the novel—'the highest form of subtle inter-relatedness'. Pasternak in describing Yury's and Lara's love sets it against 'the whole spectacle, the whole universe'. Not only are human lives mysteriously linked, but in the supreme moments of history 'stars and trees come together and converse, flowers at night talk philosophy and stone edifices hold meetings'. It is 'something evangelical . . . As in the time of the apostles' (V, 8). Pasternak has noted that two modern poets, Mayakovsky and Esenin, drew freely on the imagery and language of the Church for their own uses.[3] He was glad that they

> did not pass by what they had known and remembered from childhood, that they turned up this soil of custom, and exploited the beauty contained in it . . .

Doctor Zhivago begins with the chanting at a funeral service:

They went on and on and sang 'Eternal memory', and when they paused it seemed that the singing was kept up in unison by the feet, the horses, the gusts of wind.

At one point the activity of the poet who 'continually reflects on death and continually thereby creates life' (III, 17) is linked with the Book of Revelations. Prophecy and commemoration are the twin poles of Pasternak's novel, which ends in Moscow, the city that becomes 'principal heroine of the long story' and unites past, present and future. The prophecy spells freedom, the premonition of which

> was borne in the air all through the postwar years and constituted their sole historical meaning.
>
> (XVI, 5)

The commemoration takes in not only Russia before the Revolution—Russia of the earnest seekers after truth like Vedenyapin, of the hospitable and easy-going Sventitskys (whose Christmas tree symbolizes the old Moscow) and of the insidious Komarovsky and the unbalanced millionaire Andrey Zhivago. It also reaches back to the days of the medieval chronicles and Russian paganism before them, in an old woman's muddled incantations. The witch Kubarikha (XII, 6, 7) would have delighted Pilnyak; his care for vanishing tradition—and Leskov's—is manifest in other parts of the novel too, which has for its opening scene a monastery graveyard, and everywhere holds on to the past —in the scent of lime trees from an ancient garden, in the antiquity of the great highway through Siberia, and the Holy Week service at a monastery beside it; in the old Russian song of Kubarikha which is like water behind a dam, seeming still but moving from beneath; in the primeval forest, and in Moscow 'the holy city'.

Doctor Zhivago appears at this point of time to close a tradition. It is—for the present—the last Russian classic, a repository of themes, attitudes and tones from which the contemporary world (and not only in Russia) has turned away. This makes it a great valedictory work, a singing of 'Eternal memory' not to a social order but to a moment of promise, in the summer of 1917, which was never fulfilled. But the theme, the pathos of all its seventeen chapters, is resurrection. Mandelshtam said that Pasternak's verse was like the German Bible of Luther to those who had read only the Vulgate. His prose in *Doctor Zhivago* 'cleanses the doors of perception'; the language once again feels with its finger tips; meanings are brought back from exile. *Doctor Zhivago* may be called a grammar of feeling, which rehearses every mode available to a mind expressing itself in Russian. This compendious work of a lifetime proves that the ways are still open, that the restraint Yury so much admired in Pushkin and Chekhov, and the passionate directness of Tolstoy, can be won back given the right conditions. They depend upon freedom as Pasternak himself practised it, a freedom that involves constant sacrifice and is very difficult to attain. In the Russian imagination we have seen two principles contending for mastery: the first (in its extreme form) represented by Oblomov; the second by Ivan Karamazov. Sensibility and will; acceptance and denial; humility and pride; spontaneity and control—the opposition can take many forms. It is the interplay of these tendencies that has kept the Russian genius perennially active. Pasternak alone in our day has made his mind their arena. The victory of Yury Zhivago rather than Strelnikov restores the balance. In the circumstances Yury, the stone that the builders rejected, was chosen to become the keystone of a new arch. But *Doctor Zhivago* will not always remain the last Russian classic. One great work answers and corrects another. What Pasternak has achieved by his solitary master-piece is to ensure that the debate will continue.[4]

Notes and references

Introduction

1. M. Arnold, 'Count Leo Tolstoi' (1887), *Essays in Criticism, Second Series*
2. D. H. Lawrence, *Studies in Classic American Literature* (1923), Foreword
   See also G. Steiner, *Tolstoy or Dostoevsky* (1959), pp. 30–41
3. N. G. Chernyshevsky, *Ocherki gogolevskogo perioda russkoy literatury*, IX (1856)
4. F. M. Dostoevsky, *Dnevnik pisatelya*, January 1877
5. R. W. B. Lewis, *The American Adam* (1955), pp. 1–10; M. Turnell, *The Novel in France* (1962 edn.), pp. 424–31

PART ONE

Chapter 1

1. 'Neskol'ko slov o Pushkine' (1832)
2. R. Freeborn, *Turgenev: The Novelist's Novelist* (1960), p. 20
3. Speech at the unveiling of the memorial to Pushkin in Moscow, 1880
4. H. James, Preface to *The Reverberator*
5. B. Eichenbaum, *Leo Tolstoy:semidesyatye gody* (Leningrad, 1960), pp. 174–88
6. See D. Davie, *The Heyday of Sir Walter Scott* (1961), ch.ii

Chapter 3

1. Letter to Pauline Viardot, February 1852
2. *N. V. Gogol'v russkoy kritike i vospominaniyakh sovremennikov* (Moscow, 1959), pp. 286–92
3. V. Nabokov, *Nikolai Gogol* (1947), pp. 67–77
4. S. Johnson, *Rasselas*, ch. xliii

PART TWO

A note on the critics

1. Letter to Ya. P. Polonsky, 16/28-iv-1869

2. M. Arnold, *On Translating Homer*, 1861
3. A. Trollope, *An Autobiography* (Oxford, 1923), p. 198

Chapter 4
1. R. Poggioli, *The Phoenix and the Spider* (1957), p. 47

Chapter 5
1. H. James, 'Turgenev and Tolstoy' (in *The House of Fiction*, ed. Leon Edel, 1957).
2. Do., 'Ivan Turgénieff', *French Poets and Novelists* (1884)
3. Do., 'Daniel Deronda: A Conversation', *Partial Portraits* (1888)
4. N. A. Dobrolyubov, '*Kogda zhe pridyot nastoyashchiy den*'?' (1860)
5. Letter to K. K. Sluchevsky, 26-iv-1862 (N. S.)
6. M. Arnold, 'Heinrich Heine', *Essays in Criticism* (1865), p.155
7. Letter to Herzen, 28-iv-1862 (N.S.)
8. H. James, Preface to *The Portrait of a Lady*

Chapter 6
1. Letter to M. A. Protopopov, 23-xii-1891

Chapter 7
1. F. Venturi, *Roots of Revolution* (1960), pp. 354–88
2. See V. Zhdanov, *Tvorcheskaya istoriya Anny Kareninoy* (Moscow, 1957)
3. See p. 24.
4. B. Eichenbaum, *op. cit.*, pp. 83–5
5. For an exchange on this subject see H. Gifford, 'Anna, Lawrence and the Law'; Raymond Williams, 'Lawrence and Tolstoy'; H. Gifford, 'Further Notes on *Anna Karenina*': in *Critical Quarterly*, I, iii; II, i and ii (1959–60)
6. M. Arnold, 'Count Leo Tolstoi' (1887), *Essays in Criticism, Second Series*
7. N. G. Chernyshevsky, '*Detstvo, Otrochestvo . . . Voennye rasskazy grafa L. N. Tolstogo*' (1857)
8. B. Eichenbaum, *op. cit.*, pp. 207–18
9. M. Arnold, *op. cit.*

Chapter 8
1. From notes of a conversation in 1881, *q.* I. S. Turgenev, *Sobranie sochineniy* (Moscow, 1956) XI, p. 497

Chapter 9

1. F. Venturi, *op. cit.*, p. 79
2. F. M. Dostoevsky, *Dnevnik pisatelya*, July–August 1877
3. V. V. Rozanov, *Legenda o velikom inkvisitore*, 1890
4. A. Gide, *Dostoïevski* (Paris, 1923), p. 61
5. N. A. Dobrolyubov, '*Zabitye Lyudi*', 1861
6. S. A. Vengerov, q. in *F. M. Dostoevskiy, Pis'ma*, IV (Moscow 1959), p. 372
7. H. James, 'The Life of George Eliot', *Partial Portraits* (1888), p. 52
8. As reported by Dostoevsky in *Dnevnik pisatelya*, January 1877
9. N. Berdyaev, *Dostoievsky* (1934), ch. ix
10. Preface to *The Grand Inquisitor*, in *Selected Literary Criticism*, ed. A. Beal (1955), p. 235

PART THREE

A note on the beginning of modern times

1. See V. G. Korolenko, 'Vsevolod Mikhaylovich Garshin', *Sobranie sochineniy* (Moscow, 1955), VIII, pp. 220, 247
2. *Op. cit.*, pp. 227–8
3. Ch. xxxviii

Chapter 10

1. J. Middleton Murry, *Discoveries* (1924), p. 76
2. Letter to Rhys Davies, 25-xii-1928
3. E. Wilson, *To the Finland Station* (1960 edn.), p. 356 f
4. *Literaturnoe nasledstvo*, vol. 68, 'Chekhov' (Moscow, 1960), pp. 133–40
5. Tatyana Shchepkina–Kupernik: 'O Chekhove', *A. P. Chekhov v vospominaniyakh sovremennikov* (Moscow, 1947), p. 202

Chapter 11

1. L. E. Obolensky, *Maksim Gor'kiy i prichiny ego uspekha* (St Petersburg, 1903)
2. See ch. XIV, pp. 176 ff

Chapter 12

1. Letter to Saltykov-Shchedrin, 25-xi-1875 (N.S.)

2. K. Mochulsky, *Andrey Belyy* (Paris, 1955)
3. Do., *Aleksandr Blok* (Paris, 1948), pp. 323–7

Chapter 13

1. E. Zamyatin, 'Novaya russkaya proza', *Litsa* (New York, 1955)
2. *Op. cit.*, 'Zakulisy'. Cf. 'On Literature, Revolution and Entropy', *Partisan Review*, 3–4, 1961
3. K. Paustovsky, 'Reminiscences of Babel', *Partisan Review*, 3–4, 1961
4. V. V. Mayakovsky, 'Bez belykh flagov', 1914

Chapter 14

1. Ch. xi, pp. 138–9
2. L. Trotsky, *Literature and Revolution*, ch. vi
3. G. Santayana, *Soliloquies in England* (1922), p. 65
4. M. Hayward, 'Introduction. Soviet Literature, 1917–1961', *Partisan Review*, 3–4, 1961, p. 350
5. O. Mandelshtam, 'Barsuch'ya nora', *Sobranie sochineniy* (New York, 1955), p. 359

Chapter 15

1. Stuart Hampshire in *Encounter*, November 1958, suggested that the method of *Doctor Zhivago* is Shakespearian. Pasternak knew Shakespeare intimately from his work on translation, and the hint discloses affinities which seem hardly less important than those with Pushkin, Tolstoy and Chekhov.
2. The originals hung on the wall of Pasternak's study. Gerd Ruge, 'A Visit to Pasternak', *Encounter*, March 1958
3. B. Pasternak, *An Essay in Autobiography* (1959), ch. iv
4. I have also written on *Doctor Zhivago* in vol. IX of *Essays in Criticism* (April 1959), pp. 159–70.

Select bibliograhpy

A. General Works

Janko Lavrin, *An Introduction to the Russian Novel* (Methuen, 1942)

Georg Lukács, *Studies in European Realism* (Hillway, 1950)

D. S. Mirsky, *A History of Russian Literature*, ed. and abridged by Francis J. Whitfield (Routledge, 1960)

Gilbert Phelps, *The Russian Novel in English Fiction* (Hutchinson, 1956)

V. S. Pritchett, *The Living Novel* (Chatto and Windus, 1946)

George Reavey, *Soviet Literature Today* (Drummond, 1946)

Gleb Struve, *25 Years of Soviet Literature 1918–1943* (Routledge, 1944)

Leon Trotsky, *Literature and Revolution*, tr. Rose Strunsky (Michigan, 1960)

Franco Venturi, *Roots of Revolution* (Weidenfeld & Nicolson, 1960)

B. Studies of Particular Authors, and some Translations

ANDREEV

Maxim Gorky, *Reminiscences of Tolstoy, Chekhov and Andreev*, tr. Katherine Mansfield, S. S. Koteliansky and Leonard Woolf (Hogarth Press, 1934), pp. 117–91

BABEL

Konstantin Paustovsky, 'Reminiscences of Babel', *Partisan Review*, 3–4, 1961

Renato Poggioli, *The Phoenix and the Spider* (Cambridge, Mass., 1957), pp. 229–38

Collected Stories, tr. Walter Morison, with Introduction by Lionel Trilling (Penguin, 1961)

BELY

St Petersburg, tr. J. Cournos (Weidenfeld & Nicolson, 1960)

BUNIN

Renato Poggioli, *The Phoenix and the Spider* (Cambridge, Mass., 1957), pp. 131–57

'The Gentleman from San Francisco', tr. D. H. Lawrence and

S. S. Kotel. nsky in *Russian Short Stories* (Penguin, 1941)
Shadowed Paths [nine stories including 'The Gentleman from San Francisco' and '*Sukhodol*'] (Moscow, 1961)

CHEKHOV

W. H. Bruford, *Anton Chekhov* (Bowes and Bowes, 1957)
Maxim Gorky, *Reminiscences of Tolstoy, Chekhov and Andreev*, tr. Katherine Mansfield, S. S. Kotel. nsky and Leonard Woolf (Hogarth Press, 1934), pp. 91–111
Plays and Stories, tr. S. S. Kotel. nsky (Dent: Everyman's Library, 1937)
The Tales of Tchehov, tr. Constance Garnett (Chatto and Windus, 1916–22)

DOSTOEVSKY

Nicholas Berdyaev, *Dostoievsky* (Sheed & Ward, 1936)
E. H. Carr, *Dostoevsky (1821–1881)* (Allen & Unwin, 1931)
André Gide, *Dostoevsky* (Dent, 1926)
Ronald Hingley, *The Undiscovered Dostoyevsky* (Hamish Hamilton, 1962)
D. H. Lawrence, *Selected Literary Criticism*, ed. Anthony Beal (Heinemann, 1955), pp. 229–41
E. J. Simmons, *Dostoevski: The Making of a Novelist* (New York, 1940)
George Steiner, *Tolstoy or Dostoevsky* (Faber, 1959)
The Brothers Karamazov, tr. Constance Garnett (Dent: Everyman's Library, 1927)
The Brothers Karamazov, tr. David Magarshack (Penguin, 1958)

GARSHIN

The Scarlet Flower [with ten other stories] (Moscow, 1961)

GOGOL

David Magarshack, *Gogol: A Life* (Faber, 1957)
Vladimir Nabokov, *Nikolai Gogol* (Poetry London, 1947)
Dead Souls, tr. David Magarshack (Penguin, 1961)

GONCHAROV

Renato Poggioli, *The Phoenix and the Spider* (Cambridge, Mass., 1957), pp. 33–48
Oblomov, tr. Natalie Duddington (Dent: Everyman's Library, 1932)
Oblomov, tr. David Magarshack (Penguin, 1954)

GORKY

Richard Hare, *Maxim Gorky: Romantic Realist and Conservative Revolutionary* (O.U.P., 1962)

Helen Muchnic, *From Gorky to Pasternak* (Methuen, 1963), pp. 29–103

Childhood, tr. M. Wettlin, revised by J. Coulson (O.U.P: World's Classics, 1961)

Foma Gordeyev, tr. Margaret Wetlin (Lawrence and Wishart, 1956)

The Artamonov Business, tr. Alec Brown (Hamish Hamilton, 1948)

ILF and PETROV

The Twelve Chairs, tr. J. H. C. Richardson (New York, 1961)

The Golden Calf, tr. J. H. C. Richardson (Frederick Muller, 1964)

LEONOV

Helen Muchnic, *From Gorky to Pasternak* (Methuen, 1963), pp. 276–303

LERMONTOV

A Hero of Our Own Times, tr. Eden and Cedar Paul (O.U.P.: World's Classics, 1958)

LESKOV

Cathedral Folk, tr. I. F. Hapgood (Lane, 1924)

Selected Tales of Nikolai Leskov, tr. D. Magarshack, with Introduction by V. S. Pritchett (Secker and Warburg, 1962)

PASTERNAK

Olga Carlisle, 'Three Visits with Boris Pasternak', *The Paris Review*, Summer-Fall, 1960

Stuart Hampshire,' "Doctor Zhivago": As from a lost culture', *Encounter*, November 1958

Helen Muchnic, *From Gorky to Pasternak* (Methuen, 1963), pp. 341–404

Edmund Wilson, 'Doctor Life and His Guardian Angel', *The New Yorker*, 15 November 1958

Doctor Zhivago, tr. Max Hayward and Manya Harari (Collins and Harvill Press, 1958)

An Essay in Autobiography, tr. Manya Harari (Collins and Harvill Press, 1959)

PILNYAK

Mahogany, tr. Max Hayward, *Partisan Review*, 3–4, 1961

The Naked Year, tr. A. Brown (London, 1928)

PUSHKIN

Donald Davie, *The Heyday of Sir Walter Scott* (Routledge, 1961), pp. 1–11

Edmund Wilson, *The Triple Thinkers* (Lehmann, 1952), pp. 37–63

The Captain's Daughter and Other Stories, tr. Natalie Duddington (Dent: Everyman's Library, 1933)

The Captain's Daughter and The Negro of Peter the Great, tr. Rosemary Edmonds (London: Spearman, 1958)

The Queen of Spades [and other stories], tr. Rosemary Edmonds (Penguin, 1962)

SALTYKOV-SHCHEDRIN

The Golovlyov Family, tr. Natalie Duddington (Dent: Everyman's Library, 1934)

SHOLOKHOV

Helen Muchnic, *From Gorky to Pasternak* (Methuen, 1963), pp. 304–40

And Quiet Flows The Don, tr. Stephen Garry (Four Square Books, 1957)

The Don Flows Home To The Sea, tr. Stephen Garry (Four Square Books, 1960)

Virgin Soil Upturned, tr. Stephen Garry (Ace Books, 1961)

SOLOGUB

The Little Demon, tr. Ronald Wilks (Four Square Books, 1962)

TOLSTOY

Isaiah Berlin, *The Hedgehog and The Fox* (Weidenfeld & Nicolson, 1953)

Maxim Gorky *Reminiscences of Tolstoy, Chekhov and Andreev*, tr. Katherine Mansfield, S. S. Koteliansky and Leonard Woolf (Hogarth Press, 1934), pp. 13–84

Thomas Mann, *Essays of Three Decades*, tr. H. T. Lowe-Porter (Secker and Warburg, n.d.), pp. 176–88

Aylmer Maude, *The Life of Tolstoy* (O.U.P.: World's Classics, 1930)

Renato Poggioli, *The Phoenix and the Spider* (Cambridge, Mass., 1957), pp. 49–108

E. J. Simmons, *Leo Tolstoy* (London, 1949)

George Steiner, *Tolstoy or Dostoevsky* (Faber, 1959)

Lionel Trilling, *The Opposing Self* (Secker and Warburg, 1955), pp. 66–75

Anna Karenina, tr. Rosemary Edmonds (Penguin, 1954)

TURGENEV

Richard Freeborn, Turgenev: *The Novelist's Novelist* (O.U.P., 1960)

Henry James, *French Poets and Novelists* (London, 1884), pp. 211–52

Henry James, *Partial Portraits* (London, 1888), pp. 291–323

Henry James, *The House of Fiction*, ed. Leon Edel (Hart-Davis, 1957), pp. 168–75

Fathers and Children, tr. Constance Garnett (Heinemann, 1928)

Fathers and Children, tr. Avril Pyman (Dent: Everyman's Library, 1962)

ZAMYATIN

D. J. Richards, *Zamyatin: A Soviet Heretic* (Bowes and Bowes, 1962)

'On Literature, Revolution and Entropy', *Partisan Review*, 3–4, 1961

We, tr. G. Zilboorg (New York, 1959)

We in *Anthology of Soviet Stories*, ed. B. Guerney (New York, 1959)

ZOSHCHENKO

Scenes From The Bath-house, and Other Stories of Communist Russia, tr. Sidney Monas (Cresset, 1963)

Nervous People and Other Satires, tr. M. Gordon and H. McLean (London, 1963)

Index

The most important page references are in italic.

HARPER COLOPHON BOOKS